MORE ADVENTURES WITH
LEADERS AND ENDERS

MAKE EVEN **MORE** QUILTS IN LESS TIME
BONNIE K. HUNTER

MAKE EVEN **MORE** QUILTS IN LESS TIME

BONNIE K. HUNTER

MORE ADVENTURES WITH
LEADERS AND ENDERS

Editor | Jenifer Dick
Designer | Brian Grubb
Photography | Aaron T. Leimkuehler
Illustration | Eric Sears
Technical Editors | Nan Doljac and Jane Miller
Photo Editor | Jo Ann Groves

Published by:
Kansas City Star Books
1729 Grand Blvd.
Kansas City, Missouri, USA 64108

All rights reserved
Copyright © 2014 Bonnie K. Hunter and
The Kansas City Star Co.

No part of this book may be reproduced, stored
in a retrieval system, or transmitted in any form
or by any means, electronic, mechanical,
photocopying, recording or otherwise, without
the prior consent of the publisher. Exception:
we grant permission to photocopy the patterns
for personal use only.

No designs, finished quilts, or other projects
featured in this book can be produced or sold
commercially without the permission of the
author and publisher.

First edition, Second Printing
ISBN: 978-1-61169-124-5

Library of Congress Control Number:
2014933642

Printed in the United States of America by
Walsworth Publishing Co., Marceline, MO

MAKE EVEN **MORE** QUILTS IN LESS TIME
BONNIE K. HUNTER

To order copies, call StarInfo at (816) 234-4473.

KANSAS CITY STAR QUILTS
Continuing the Tradition

PickleDish.com
The Quilter's Home Page

DEDICATION

If you had asked me a mere six years ago where I would envision my life today, I would never have guessed in my wildest dreams that it would be where it is today.

Six years ago I was working as a licensed neuromuscular massage therapist in South Carolina with no thought of giving up my practice or even thinking of publishing books on quilting. Oh, quilting was going on full-force alright – I have been a fabric fiend since I was 18 years old - but it was my pleasure, my release, my pastime. But a career in writing?

Today I sit and reflect how much has changed on this crazy journey as an itinerant traveling, book writing quilter who is no longer a massage therapist, but is loving life and all the twists and turns and tangents it throws at my feet.

Dare to dream. Never say never. Don't be afraid to let go of things just because they are comfortable. And don't focus on the end of the road because it might lead somewhere different, somewhere even better than you thought! Just be on that road and marvel at each step along the way. And always, always, always follow your bliss.

ACKNOWLEDGEMENTS

As with previous releases, I owe this all to my family who support and encourage me as well as put up with long absences while I travel and teach nationally and internationally, sharing my love of traditional, scrappy quilts with quilters both in person and through this life-changing vehicle called the Internet.

To you, my readers, my family and friends – thank you for pushing me forward and encouraging me in my passion to keep playing with my fabric scraps with reckless abandon. There is NO stopping this train!

More Adventures with Leaders & Enders is my sixth publication with the great folks at Kansas City Star Books. My complete and heartfelt thanks go to the entire staff who feel more like close friends and family after this amount of time.

I'd like to thank the team that helped put this book together: Brian Grubb, Aaron Leimkuehler, Nan Doljac and Jane Miller, Jo Ann Groves and Eric Sears. Special thanks to Jenifer Dick for tackling NUMBER SIX with me, in between writing her own Kansas City Star books and being a very busy mom herself – thanks friend!

Remember, if it's still UGLY, you just didn't cut it SMALL ENOUGH!

– Bonnie K. Hunter

FOREWORD

Five years have passed since the release of **Adventures with Leaders & Enders.** Why so long of a wait for a sequel? Because the whole premise of sewing with Leaders & Enders is about building units in between the lines of chain piecing other things, one at a time – it is not a race. Units build on the side, one by one and then, almost like magic, there are enough units for a wall hanging, a baby quilt, a lap quilt or even a bed quilt.

The basics of working with Leaders & Enders are simple, yet it was life changing for me in terms of productivity and organization.

With the release of **More Adventures with Leaders & Enders,** I am even more convinced that we can make better use of our time, our fabric, our thread just by implementing this one simple method of always leaving a pair of something underneath the presser foot when we end a line of chain piecing.

Do I have your attention? Are you curious to know more? Continue reading and we will have you hooked in no time at all. Your own adventure with Leaders & Enders is just about to begin!

May you always find one more unit to leave under the presser foot of your machine as you chain piece!

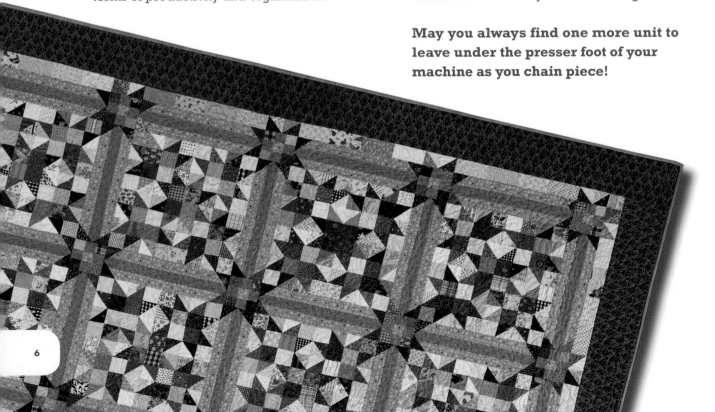

CONTENTS

PROJECTS

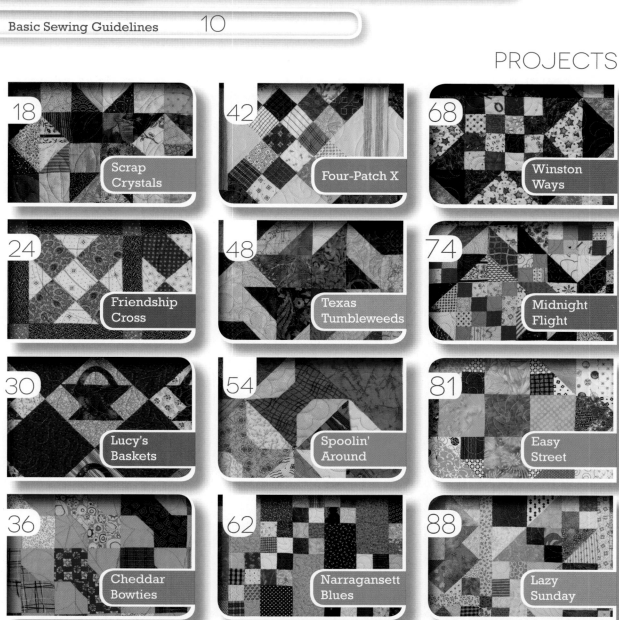

JUST WHAT ARE LEADERS AND ENDERS?

A long time ago, I learned to use a folded scrap to sew on and off of at the beginning or ending of a line of chain piecing leaving the scrap underneath my presser foot and snipping the threads between it and my piecing behind. This always leaves something under the foot so I don't start the next line of piecing with long threads getting tangled or sucked down the needle hole pulling my fabric pieces with it. Or worse yet, having to trim all those long threads, trying to get them into the trash, but finding them more often on the floor, clogging the wheels of my wheelie chair at my sewing machine as I roll over them, or tangled around the vacuum beater bar!

This is how it worked: When chain piecing, as I got to the end of the line and it was time to remove the work from the machine to press the units, I put another fabric scrap through the machine and trimmed behind it to keep the piecing as continuous as possible. When I got up to the top of the piecing I just trimmed off, I removed the fabric scrap (sometimes called a thread-bunny, spider or sew-between by those who use this method) and had it ready for ending the next line of piecing.

I typically had two "sew-betweens" going at any given time – one under the foot as the "Leader" to start the piecing and the next one to be the "Ender" as I ended the piecing. The "Ender" becomes the new "Leader" as I start the next line of piecing.

I continued to use the same scraps to sew on and off of until they were clogged with thread, and they would still end up in the trash. I started with new ones until they were too full of thread to use anymore.

Then a light bulb went off. What if I took a bin of scrap 2" squares that had been accumulating from trimming scraps down, and start using pairs of those as Leaders & Enders instead of a wadded-up thread-covered scrap? I sewed a light square to a dark square with my regular $1/4$" seam, trimmed off behind it and eventually had a stack of little "two-sies" that I could also use to sew into four patches. And my adventures with Leaders & Enders began!

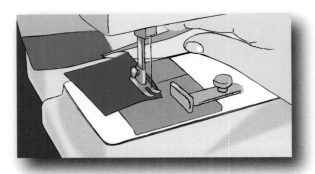

Leader & Ender pair under the presser foot, thread snips separating work by clipping behind the Leader & Ender pair.

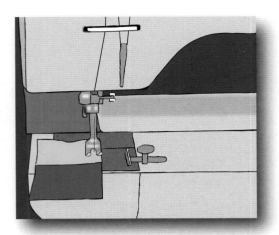

A pair of "twoosies" being sewn into a four-patch as a Leader & Ender unit following a line of chain piecing.

I soon learned that anything can be a Leader & Ender. In this book I have used 2" squares, both in scrappy with all colors, as shown in the **Narragansett Blues** quilt found on page 62 as well as 2" squares from cheddar solid and a variety of scraps in **Cheddar Bowties** on page 36, or even odd shapes as in **Friendship Cross** found on page 24. There are quilts using 1 ½" squares and even some using rectangles, as found in **Spoolin' Around** on page 54.

The premise is simple. All you have to do is think ahead far enough to have pieces cut and sitting by your machine so you are ready to have something to feed through in between your lines of chain piecing.

What about that pieced border for the quilt you are already making? Who wants to leave the pieced border for the very end of the quilt? What if you took those pieces for that border, had them all cut and ready to go sitting at the side of your machine? While you are chain piecing on the quilt top, use the border pieces as Leaders & Enders and you will have that border sewn together and ready to attach to your quilt without having to stress about it! Consider doing this for quilts in this book, especially **Lazy Sunday** found on page 88.

How about that UFO that's been sitting in a box on your shelf for three years or more because you couldn't make yourself want to work on it? Take those unloved pieces. Put them by your machine. As you are piecing on something you want to be piecing, use those UFO pieces as your Leaders & Enders and your UFO will piece itself without you having to beat yourself up about it. That's a great feeling!

Leaders & Enders can be any shape - squares, rectangles, diamonds, triangles, even strips - it just takes a bit of planning.

Did you know it takes 21 days to create a habit? Sewing with Leaders & Enders might feel strange at first, but after a while you will find yourself automatically grabbing for something to feed into the machine before removing your chain piecing for pressing. And, it's a good habit to have — no wasted thread, lots of bonus units for quilts and more quilts sewn in between the lines of chain piecing other quilts.

Leader & Ender projects can spend a long time in between other quilts to build up enough units until you have enough to make a full sized project. Sometimes Leader & Ender projects will nag at you wanting to become a primary project! And that is okay, too. For those of you who want to get a jump start on the projects in this book, you will find instructions starting on page 12 showing how to quickly piece the four-patch and other units in fast order so you can use other pieces as your Leaders & Enders in between the quick piecing.

The patterns for the quilts in this book are based on rotary cutting and machine piecing methods. It is assumed that the reader has a basic knowledge of quilting techniques and processes. The tools used are also the same as in basic quilt making. To avoid frustration, it is necessary to have a sewing machine in good working order. Only a straight stitch is required. There are a few additional tips I've picked up along the way to make my quilt making easier and faster, and I'd like to share them with you.

That ¼" seam allowance

It is important to find where the ¼" seam is on your machine. If you can master this, all your blocks will be the same size and you'll be able to match points perfectly. Even if your machine foot has a ¼" guide on it, it is easy to over-shoot your ¼" seam just by the nature of that guide already being "outside" of your ¼" foot. We have a habit of running the fabric too hard up against the guide giving us a seam that is way too wide. Do not trust ANY feet with "built-in" guides until you do a seam test!

Sew 2 – 2 ½" squares together with your best ¼" seam and press. These two units sewn together should measure 4 ½" side-by-side. Measure them by placing your rotary ruler ON TOP of the unit. Numbers don't lie! If your unit is less than 4 ½", your seam allowance needs a diet! If your unit measures

more than 4 ½" it needs to fatten up a bit. Do what you have to do to fix the seam so your units come out the size they are supposed to before going any further. You and your quilt will be glad you did!

The Scrap User's System

As a longtime scrap quilter, I needed a method that would help keep my scraps readily available for ease in making scrap quilts. I much prefer to be sitting and sewing than pressing and cutting from odd-size scraps.

If I could tackle the leftover scraps from each project as I made them, they'd be ready for me to sew any time I had time.

Most of the quilts in this book come from common sizes of units used to make each block. Units are usually created by combining pre-cut squares, or cutting triangles and other units out of already-cut strips. These are sizes of strips we use all the time in traditional patchwork. They all came from my own Scrap User's System of storing strips in useable sizes so they are ready to go. By precutting my scraps and storing them by size and value or color family, I have the ease of pulling the perfect size and color so I can just sit and sew. It's a scrap user's dream!

Scrap Strip Sizes

I cut fabric pieces that are at least 10" to 12" long into 1 1/2", 2", 2 1/2" and 3 1/2" widths. I don't cut new yardage off fat quarters this way, just the scraps that are leftover from whatever project I am working on.

These strips are stored by color and value in plastic stackable drawers that live under the table of my longarm quilting machine. There are drawers for each strip width.

Within each size-labeled drawer I have sorted each strip width into color families. For example, in my 2 1/2" strip bin you will find each color bundle – blue, green, red, purple, orange, brown, etc. Strips are stacked and rolled in an oblong bundle (think hot-dog bun instead of jelly-roll) with each color family being placed in a gallon zipper seal plastic bag to contain them. This keeps them wrinkle free, and edges do not get thready and tangled.

For example, I easily pulled the bag of 2 1/2" blue strips and the bag of 2 1/2" neutral strips for making the half-square triangles for **Winston Ways,** found on page 68.

Before I started sorting strips by color, I would have to dig through everything just to find the color I was searching for.

Smaller fabric pieces and short strips less than 10" to 12" in length are cut into individual squares and bricks by strip width.

1 1/2" squares and 1 1/2" x 2 1/2" bricks

2" squares and 2" x 3 1/2" bricks

2 1/2" squares and 2 1/2" x 4 1/2" bricks

3 1/2" squares

These shapes work great together – using the sew-and-flip method you have everything you need at hand to create flying geese units and star point units as Leaders & Enders. Just put the squares and bricks by your machine and start building units!

Simple squares are the starting point for scrappy four-patches and nine-patches built as Leaders & Enders as well.

Where else can you use pre-cut squares in a variety of sizes? How about block corners, block centers, cornerstones for sashing and even checkerboard borders? The list is endless.

Anything that is too small or oddly shaped to work as a pre-cut strip is delegated to my string bins. String piecing is another passion - check out my book **String Fling** to find out how to use those.

Neutrals v. Colors

When working on a scrap quilt – especially one that uses a lot of busy fabrics in every color under the rainbow with a whole lot of variety going on – I tend to keep my backgrounds with less color than the foregrounds.

I love a wide variety of neutrals in a neutral-background quilt. Most of the time when I am thinking "lights" I am thinking mostly in terms of neutrals – white to cream to beige to tan - with some pastels thrown in that are very light – pink, yellow, blue, green, etc. But they have to be very pale if I am going to use them in a light-toned scrappy background. Look at the fabric's ground (its background). That will tell you where it wants to play. For instance, a cream fabric with blue flowers and green leaves will qualify as a background neutral because of the cream ground of the fabric. Black music notes on white? It's a neutral because of the white background. Focus on the ground, not on the print.

How dark will I go on neutrals? Keep in mind the color of a brown paper bag – if I am using many shades of neutral as a background – brown paper bag color is as dark as I will go. If I go darker than that, it has become darker than medium - it has crossed over to the foreground side.

I think of "darks" more as colors. They are everything that is not light. That means most mediums read as dark against the neutral lights to me, and I will kick mediums to the other side to play their part in the main design as foreground.

FOUR-PATCH UNITS

When you reach the end of a line of chain piecing and it is time for pressing, grab two squares from beside your machine. Match them with right sides together and sew with a ¼" seam. Leave these pieces under the presser foot and remove your work by snipping the threads between your patchwork and your Leader/Ender squares behind the presser foot. Start your next line of chain piecing, ending with another pair of Leader/Ender squares. Start a stack of these little "two-sies." When you have enough of them, you can join them together into four-patch blocks by matching the pairs together as Leaders & Enders when you reach the end of another line of chain piecing on whatever project you are working on.

I keep the Leader/Ender four patches in a basket, pinned in sets of 10 so they are always close at hand when I need them for borders, blocks, cornerstones and anywhere else a four patch unit can be used.

HALF SQUARE TRIANGLES

When piecing half-square triangles in Leader & Ender style, I match the two fabrics right sides together and cut the triangles, usually with the Easy Angle Ruler (See page 15) so the pairs are already matched. I do all the matching of what is going to be sewn next to what in the cutting process so when I sit at the machine, it is easy to feed the already matched and cut pairs through the machine as a Leader/Ender unit! Having them cut in matched pairs means less handling of the bias edges, and saves me lots of time.

SPINNING FOUR-PATCH SEAMS

Why spin the seams? It helps eliminate bulk in the center of the four patches, and in blocks where four patches join other four patches, it allows all the seams to nest automatically without fighting each other.

When sewing four patches, it is important that all of the pairs get sewn through the machine in the same direction.

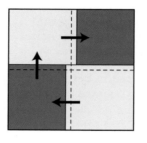 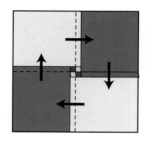

When chain piecing, send all the four-patch pairs through the machine with the dark square going under the needle first. This helps nest the opposing center seams, giving a much better join, working with the feed dogs instead of against them. To make sure I do these all uniformly, I repeat to myself "Dark Square Leading!"

After sewing, press all the seams in one direction as shown. You will have three seams rotating, and one going the wrong way.

Look at the four seams on the back of the four patch as if they are a clock face with the top seam being 12:00, the right side seam being 3:00, the bottom being 6:00, and the left side seam representing 9:00.

12:00 and 6:00 are anchored by the center seam that goes from side to side. These two seams cannot change direction.

Look at the way that 12:00 is pointing. If the seam is pointing to the right as shown, your seams are all going to circle to the right or "clockwise". If the seam was pointing to the left, your seams would circle "counterclockwise." They should be going clockwise if you sewed the pairs with the dark square leading your pair through the machine.

Bring the 3:00 seam down, giving it a gentle twist. This will allow a couple of stitches within the seam allowance to release, allowing the center to lay flat.

If the stitches are stubborn, use a seam ripper to undo a couple of stitches within that seam allowance, taking care not to cross that center seam. It is important to not back tack when joining your four patches together or this will not work. This also works best with a normal stitch length. Stitch lengths that are too small will not allow the threads to release.

After the seams are spun, give the block another good press and you are ready to go!

MAKE MINE STRIP PIECED!

Strip piecing is such a time saver. It's like doing twice as much work in half the time. If you want to make the quilts in this book without the time it takes to build them using the Leaders & Enders method, here are some basic instructions to get you started.

Basic four-patch strip piecing construction

Determine the finished size of the individual square in the four-patch you desire. Add ¹/₂" to this measurement for the seam allowance. Cut your strips this width. If you are making patterns from this book, your strips will be cut the same size as the individual Leader & Ender squares listed in the cutting instructions for each pattern.

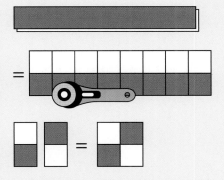

Sew the strips with right sides together, using a ¹/₄" seam. Press toward the darker fabric. Using a rotary cutter and ruler, sub-cut the strip set into the same measurement as the strips were cut. Reverse half of the units by turning them and stitch in pairs, forming the four-patch unit. Press.

The number of blocks you can get out of a strip set will vary upon the length of your strips and the desired finished size of your four-patch.

Specialty Rulers

Throughout each pattern in this book, you will find instructions for using these specialty rulers and regular rotary cutting methods for those who don't have access to these rulers.

Easy Angle Half-Square Triangles as Leaders & Enders

Determine the finished size of your half-square triangle unit and add $1/2$" for seam allowance to get the needed width of your strips. Cut strips this width.

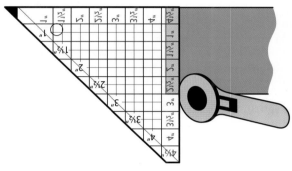

Place a light and a dark fabric strip with right sides together. Square off one end of the strip set.

Position 1: Find the number on the bottom of the ruler corresponding with the size of the strip set. Place that line on the end of the strip set. The number corresponding to the strip width should be in the upper corner of the strip (2 $1/2$" shown). Cut through both layers with a rotary cutter.

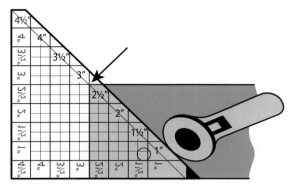

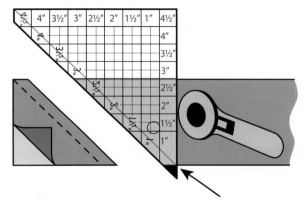

Position 2: Flip the tool over its long side (the hypotenuse), and line up the angled edge of the ruler with the cut edge of the strip-set, with the black triangle tip of the tool below the strip as shown. Cut along the edge perpendicular to the strip. Continue with these two cutting steps for additional triangles.

Stack the pairs of half-square triangles next to your machine and sew as Leaders & Enders when needed. Press. There will be only one dog ear to trim on units cut with the Easy Angle ruler.

Companion Angle Ruler

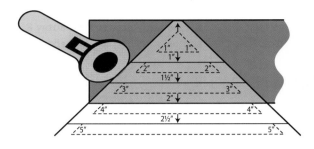 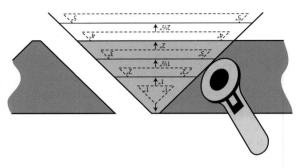

The Companion Angle ruler is used for quick cutting of quarter-square triangles from readily on-hand strips directly from my Scrap User's System. I use quarter square triangles in hour-glass units as found in Lazy Sunday on page 88 and as the "goose" part of flying geese units as found in **Easy Street** on page 81.

For the flying geese, the half-square wing triangles are cut with the Easy Angle ruler and align perfectly with the quarter-square units cut with the Companion Angle.

Find the large number indicating the finished unit size along either side of the tool. The numbers down the center of the ruler indicate the strip width you need to cut. Here, for a finished triangle base of 3", you will need to cut 2" strips.

This versatile ruler also works anywhere I want the straight grain to be on the longest side of the triangle.

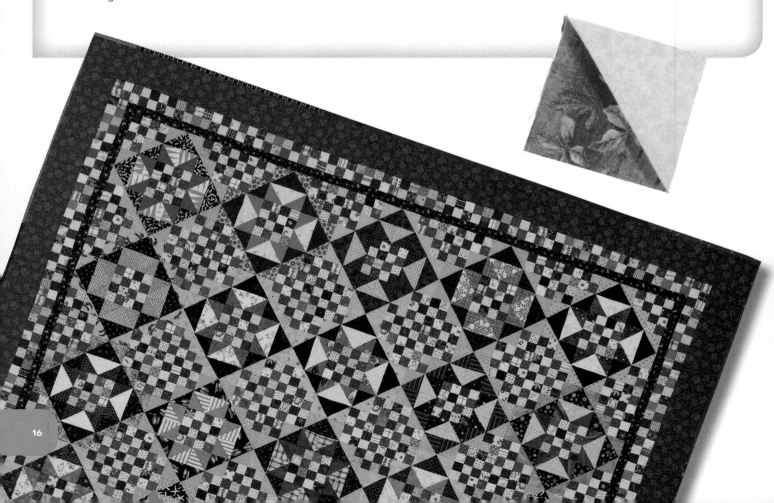

SCRAP CRYSTALS

QUILT STATISTICS
MADE BY BONNIE K. HUNTER
SIZE: 75" X 90"
BLOCKS: 20 – 12" FINISHED
PIECED INNER BORDER: 1 ¹/₂" WIDE
OUTER BORDER: 4 ¹/₂" WIDE

A box of blue and neutral bonus triangles (half-square triangles saved from other projects), a bin of 2" cut squares and a desire to sew on my 1911 treadle machine – that's all it took for me to start building simple broken dishes units as Leaders and Enders in between the lines of other projects. This is the result!

My preferred method for scrappy half-square triangles uses the Easy Angle Ruler and 2" strips for the half-square triangles in this quilt. If you wish to use any other triangle method, please do not cut your fabric into 2" strips ahead of time – this is size specific to the Easy Angle ruler. You can use any method that gives you 2" half-square triangle units that finish at 1 ¹/₂" in the quilt. With regular rotary cutting, these are generally cut from 2 ³/₈" squares.

FABRICS

Blocks and Pieced Inner Border

Note: The blocks are very scrappy - variety is important.
- 1 ¹/₃ yard total of green scraps
- 2 ¹/₂ yards total of blue scraps for star points
- 3 yards of neutral scraps for block backgrounds and pieced inner border

My neutrals include everything - small prints, plaids, stripes, shirtings, novelties and tone-on-tones all on a white, cream, beige or tan background that is no darker than paper bag brown.

Don't like blue/green? Choose any two colors that you like together to replace them, along with any background.

Sashing

- 1 ¹/₂ yards of green
- 1 yard of blue

Outer Border

- 1 ¹/₃ yards of navy

Binding

- ³/₄ yard of lime green

CUTTING

Half-Square Triangle Units

- From the blue scraps, cut 342 – 2 ³/₈" squares
- From the neutral scraps, cut 342 – 2 ³/₈" squares

If using the Easy Angle Ruler, cut blue 2" strips and neutral 2" strips.

Broken Dishes Units

- From the green scraps, cut 320 – 2" squares
- From the neutral scraps, cut 320 – 2" neutral squares

Sashing

- From the green sashing fabric, cut 34 – 1 ¹/₂" x the width of fabric strips
- From the blue sashing fabric, cut 17 – 1 ¹/₂" x the width of fabric strips
- From the blue scraps, cut 196 – 2" squares. Draw a diagonal line on the back of each square.
- From the green scraps, cut 1 ¹/₂" strips for the nine-patch cornerstones. (If using width of fabric strips, cut 8 strips.)
- From the blue scraps fabric, cut 1 ¹/₂" strips for the nine-patch cornerstones. (If using width of fabric strips, cut 8 strips.)

Inner Border

- From the neutral scraps, cut 72 – 2" x 3 ¹/₂" rectangles AND 4 – 2" squares

Outer Border

- From the navy, cut 8 – 5" x the width of fabric strips

Binding

- From the lime green, cut 10 – 2 ¹/₂" x the width of fabric strips

Diagrams are on page 22-23.

PIECING

Half-Square Triangle Units

A

Match blue and neutral 2 ³/₈" squares with right sides together and slice on the diagonal once from corner to corner yielding 684 matched pairs.

Stitch the pairs together along the bias edge and press to the blue. Trim the dog ears. The units should measure 2" and finish at 1 ¹/₂". Make 684. Reserve 44 for the inner border.

If using the Easy Angle Ruler, match a blue and neutral strip with right sides together. Using the 2" line on the ruler, cut the fabric into 684 matched pairs. Stitch the pairs together along the bias edge and press to the blue. The units should measure 2" and finish at 1 ¹/₂".

Broken Dishes Units

The Broken Dishes units are made of 1 neutral scrap 2" square, 1 green scrap 2" square and 2 blue/neutral half-square triangle units. When constructing the four patches, make sure to spin the seams as shown on page 12. This ensures that no matter what direction you turn them, the seams will always nest together.

B Arrange as shown in the diagram and sew into 320 Broken Dishes units. The units will measure 3 ¹/₂" and finish at 3" in the quilt. Make 320.

Block Quarter Unit

C Arrange 4 Broken Dishes units as shown in the diagram. Make sure 1 unit is turned with the green to the outside corner. Be sure to spin the seams as you did above. Repeat to make 80 – 6 ¹/₂" units.

Block Construction

D Join 4 block quarters with the green corner squares in the center as shown to complete each Scrap Crystals block. Press. The blocks will measure 12 ¹/₂" and finish at 12". Make 20.

Sashing

E Join the green strips on either side of the blue strips as shown in the diagram. Press to the blue strips. Cut into 49 – 3 ¹/₂" x 12 ¹/₂" sashing units.

F-G Place a blue square in the corner of the sashing unit with right sides together. Sew each square across the diagonal in a stitch-and-flip manner, covering all 4 corners on all sashing units. Trim the excess ¼" beyond the stitching line. Press the seams toward the triangles.

Nine-Patch Cornerstones

H Sew the green/blue/green and blue/green/blue strip sets. Press the seams toward the green. As I am working from scraps, my strips are all different lengths. The number of strips needed doesn't matter to me as much as the number of units I need – I just keep building scrappy strip sets until they give me the right amount.

I From the green/blue/green strip sets cut 60 units at 1 ½" intervals across the strip set.
From the blue/green/blue strip sets cut 30 units at 1 ½" intervals across the strip set.

J Arrange units and sew into 30 – nine-patch cornerstones. Press. Units will measure 3 ½" square and finish at 3" in the quilt.

Quilt Top Center Assembly

Scrap Crystals is a straight-set with sashing and ornerstones. Referring to the quilt assembly diagram on page 23 lay out the blocks, cornerstones and sashing. Stitch the quilt into rows and join the rows to complete the quilt center. Press.

Borders

Inner Border
K Inner Border Units

Join 4 - 2" x 3 ½" rectangles end to end to create one inner border to create one inner border. Press. Make 18. Units will measure 2" x 12 ½" and finish at 1 ½" x 12" in the quilt.

Star Completer Units
L Arrange 2 of the remaining blue/neutral half-square triangles as shown and stitch to make 1 star completer unit. Make 22. Press.

Arrange 2 sets of 5 inner border units and 6 star completer units and sew into border lengths for the sides of the quilt as shown in the assembly diagram. Sew 2 sets 4 inner border units, 5 star completer units and 2 – 2" squares on each end for the top and bottom inner borders. Sew to the top and bottom of the quilt top center.

Outer Border
Join the 8 navy border strips end to end on the straight of grain to make a strip approximately 320" long. Press the seams open.

Lay the quilt center out on the floor, smoothing it gently. Do not tug or pull. Measure the quilt through the center from top to bottom. Cut outer side borders this length. Sew the side borders to the quilt sides with right sides together, pinning to match centers and ends. Ease where necessary to fit. Press the seams toward the borders.

Repeat for top and bottom borders, measuring across the quilt center, including the borders just added in the measurement. Cut top and bottom borders this length. Stitch the top and bottom borders to the quilt center, pinning to match centers and ends, easing where necessary to fit. Press the seams toward the borders.

FINISHING

Scrap Crystals was quilted using beige thread in an edge-to-edge leaf design called Lots of Leaves by Hermoine Agee of Lorien Quilting, Australia. Refer to the resources page for contact information.

A lime green binding brings the myriad of greens from the quilt center to the edge of the quilt to finish.

AT A GLANCE

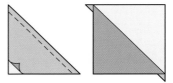

A Half-Square Triangle Units
2" square unfinished
Make 684

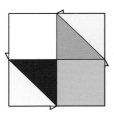

B Broken Dishes Units
3 ¹/₂" unfinished
Make 320

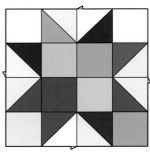

C Block Quarter Unit
6 ¹/₂" square unfinished
Make 80

D Block Assembly
12 ¹/₂" square unfinished
Make 20

E Sashing Strips – Step 1
3 ¹/₂" x 12 ¹/₂" unfinished
Make 49

F Sashing Strips – Step 2
Stitch and flip blue squares in each corner to make 4 corner triangles on each.

G Sashing Strips – Step 3
Finished Sashing Strips
Make 49

H Nine Patch Units – Step 1

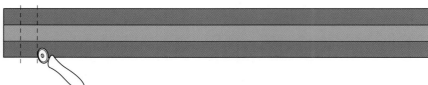

I Nine Patch Units – Step 2
Cut 60 green/blue/green – 1 ¹/₂" units
Cut 30 blue/green/blue – 1 ¹/₂" units

J Nine-Patch Cornerstones
3 ¹/₂" square unfinished
Make 30

K Inner Border Units
2" x 12 ¹/₂" unfinished
Make 18

2" x 3" unfinished
Make 22

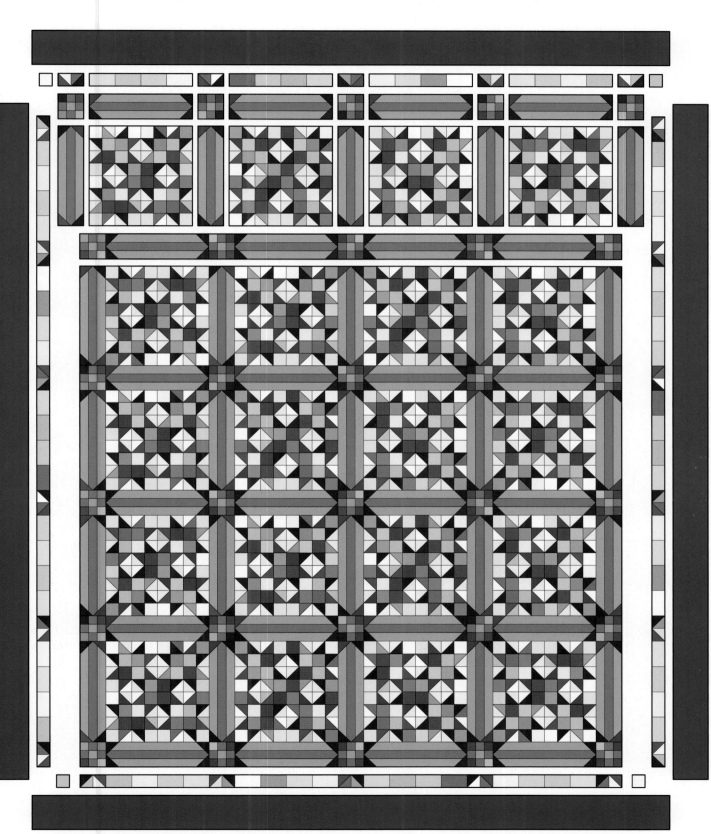

FRIENDSHIP CROSS

QUILT STATISTICS
MADE BY BONNIE K. HUNTER
SIZE: 76" X 76"
BLOCKS: 121 – 5" SQUARE FINISHED
SASHING AND CORNERSTONES: 1" WIDE FINISHED
BORDER: 4 ½" WIDE FINISHED

This quilt was made with the leftovers of the scraps used in **Lucy's Baskets** found on page 30. When faced with a short 2 ¼" strip left after cutting basket parts from scraps and sharing across the ocean with my friend, did I really want to turn those strips back into the strip bin in an odd size? NOPE! The best idea was to keep cutting them up into another project until they were gone!

The pieces cut quickly, and were pinned together in sets. They were sewn as Leaders & Enders while sewing other things and the 121 blocks were soon ready to stitch into a quilt full of friendship and memories.

FABRICS

Blocks

- 2 ¾ yards total of a variety of colored scraps. Each block in Friendship Cross uses a different print for ultimate scrappiness!
- 2 yards of a variety of neutral scraps for block backgrounds

Sashing

- 1 ⅞ yards of black mourning print
- ⅓ yard of double pink print for cornerstones

Borders

- 1 ⅜ yards of black and red print for outer border

Binding

- ¾ yard of double pink print

CUTTING

Blocks

- For each of the 121 blocks, cut 4 – 2 ¼" x 3 ¼" rectangles from the colored scraps
- For each of the 121 blocks, cut 1 – 3 ¾" square AND 1 – 2 ¼" square from the neutral scraps. Slice the large squares from corner to corner twice with an X to yield 4 background triangles

Sashing

- From the mourning print, cut 264 – 1 ½" x 5 ½" strips
- From the double pink print, cut 144 – 1 ½" x 1 ½" squares

Border

- From the black and red print, cut 8 – 5" x the width of fabric strips

Binding

- From the double pink print, cut 10 – 2 ½" x the width of fabric strips

Diagrams are on page 28-29.

PIECING

House-Shaped Units

A Trace the house-shaped template on to a piece of paper and cut out on the line. Tape the template to the backside of one corner of a small ruler as shown in the diagram.

B Stack the 4 rectangles for each block and align them with the template on the ruler. Trim the corners with a rotary cutter. Repeat for each block set.

Block Construction

C-D Lay out the block pieces and assemble the block on the diagonal in 3 rows pressing the seams to the dark fabric. Join the rows to complete the block.

Quilt Top Center Assembly

Friendship Cross is a straight-set with sashing and cornerstones. Referring to the quilt assembly diagram on page 29, lay out the blocks in 11 rows of 11 blocks each. Place the cornerstones and sashing between the rows as shown. Stitch the quilt into rows and join the rows to complete the quilt center. Press the seams toward the sashing.

Borders

Outer Border

Join the 8 border strips end to end on the straight of grain to make a strip approximately 320" long. Press the seams open.

Lay the quilt center out on the floor, smoothing it gently. Do not tug or pull. Measure the quilt through the center from top to bottom. Cut the side borders this length. Sew the borders to the quilt sides with right sides together, pinning to match centers and ends. Ease where necessary to fit. Press the seams toward the borders.

Repeat for top and bottom borders, measuring across the quilt center, including the borders just added in the measurement. Cut the top and bottom borders this length. Stitch the top and bottom borders to the quilt center, pinning to match centers and ends, easing where necessary to fit. Press the seams toward the borders.

FINISHING

Friendship Cross was machine quilted in antique gold thread with an edge to edge Baptist Fan design.

A double pink binding is a great way to tie in the pink cornerstones from the center of the quilt.

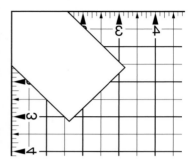

A Ruler Preparation

Cut out the house-shaped template and tape it to the back side of a small ruler.

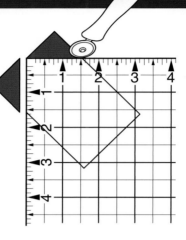

B House-Shaped Units

Make 4 for each block – 121 blocks total

C Friendship Cross Block Construction

Press to the dark

D Friendship Cross Block

5" finished
Make 121

House-Shaped Template

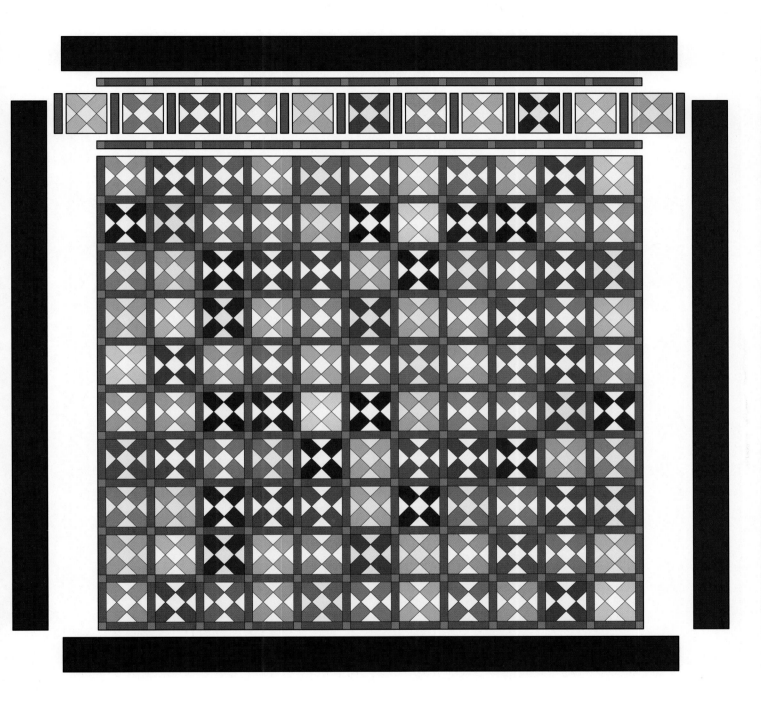

LUCY'S BASKETS

QUILT STATISTICS
MADE BY BONNIE K. HUNTER
SIZE: 70" X 85"
BASKET BLOCKS: 180 – 3 ½" FINISHED
154 SETTING BLOCKS – 3 ½" FINISHED
INNER BORDER: 1" WIDE FINISHED
OUTER PIECED BORDER: 4 ½" WIDE FINISHED

Inspired by a photo of an antique quilt, my friend Lucy invited me to swap basket "kits" with her in an effort to include each other's fabrics in our similar quilts made in friendship. This worked really well, leaving the stitching to be done by each maker, since collaborative blocks rarely turn out the same size from maker to maker!

It really IS just as easy to cut two baskets at once instead of just one from every fabric selection – one for me, one for thee – and the envelopes that crossed back and forth from her home in the Netherlands to my home here in the Carolinas were so fun to receive!

In my quilt is a special block signed to me by Lucy, and she has a block that I inscribed to her. These are the stitches and sentiments that bind our friendship together.

This is a part hand, part machine project. I kitted up the basket handle sections and kept them with me for moments of stitching while on the go to doctors' appointments, ball games and even lunch hour stitching while I was back in massage therapy school.

Once the stack of block parts was big enough, I sewed the baskets Leader and Ender style in between working on other projects. Before I knew it, I had 180 blocks ready to assemble while Lucy was here in the States visiting me.

This quilt can be made with the smallest of scraps, as each block finishes at 3 ½".

FABRICS

Blocks

- 2 yards total of dark print scraps for the baskets
- 3 yards total of light print scraps for the backgrounds

Setting Squares

- 2 ½ yards of brown print

Borders

- ½ yard of gold print for the inner border
- 2 yards of colored print scraps cut into 1 ½" strips for the pieced outer border

Binding

- ¾ yard of deep wine print

CUTTING

The cutting instructions are given to cut 2 baskets at a time. Cut 90 total for 180 blocks. See page 33 for the basket diagram and basket handle template.

Blocks

Basket Print
From 1 dark print, cut:

- 1 – 3 ½" square. Cut each square on the diagonal from corner to corner to yield 2 main basket triangles (a2).
- 2 – 1 ¾" square. Cut squares once on the diagonal to yield 4 basket feet (d).
- 2 – bias strip 1" x 4" for the basket handle (e)

Basket Background
From 1 light print, cut:

- 1 – 3 ½" square. Cut each square on the diagonal from corner to corner to yield 2 upper background triangles (a).
- 4 – 1 ⅜" x 2 ¼" rectangles (b) (2 for each basket)
- 1 – 2 ⅝" square. Cut on the diagonal from corner to corner to yield 2 background base triangles (c).

Setting Blocks and Triangles

From the brown setting fabric cut:

- 154 – 4" squares for the setting blocks
- 13 – 6 ¼" squares. Cut each twice on the diagonal with an X to yield 52 quarter-square setting triangles.

You need 50 to set the quilt, and there will be 2 left over.

- 2 – 3 ⅜ squares. Cut each once on the diagonal from corner to corner to yield 4 corner triangles.

Borders

- From the gold print, cut 8 - 1 ½" x the width of fabric strips for the inner border
- From the scraps, cut 330 – 1 ½" x 5" strips

If you choose to strip piece the border, cut scraps into 1 ½" strips. These will be sewn into panels later.

Binding

- From the wine print, cut 9 – 2 ½" x the width of fabric strips

Diagrams are on pages 33-35.

APPLIQUÉ

Block Handle

A Press each edge of the strip toward the center, overlapping the raw edges on the backside of the strip, giving a basket handle that measures approximately ⅜" wide. Using the block layout diagram, trace the handle placement to the background triangle (c).

Pin the basket handle to the upper background triangle lining up the edge with the drawn line (a1). Hand appliqué the inner curve first, then the outer curve. Press.

PIECING

Block

A Join the main basket triangle (a1) to the basket handle triangle (a2). Press the seam toward the darker fabric.

Join the basket feet triangles (d) to the side rectangles (b). Press the seams toward the triangles just added.

Join the side units to the basket. Press. Complete the block by adding the remaining (c) triangle. Press. Make 180 basket blocks. The blocks will measure 4" and finish at 3 ½".

Quilt Top Assembly

Lucy's Baskets is an on-point setting and is assembled in diagonal rows. Referring to the quilt assembly diagram on page 35, lay out the blocks and setting squares, filling in the sides with the setting triangles and corners. I like to piece on-point quilts into 2 halves.

With this quilt, one "half" will be larger than the other because it is a rectangular quilt. This keeps things from being too unwieldy, especially when sewing a large quilt top. Join quilt top halves to complete the quilt center. Press.

Borders

Inner Border
Join the 8 border strips end to end with diagonal seams to make a strip approximately 320" long. Trim the excess beyond the ¼" seam allowance and press the seams open.

Lay the quilt center out on the floor, smoothing it gently. Do not tug or pull. Measure the quilt through the center from top to bottom. Cut 2 inner side borders this length. Sew the inner side borders to the quilt sides with right sides together, pinning to match centers and ends. Ease where necessary to fit. Press the seams toward the borders.

Repeat for top and bottom inner borders, measuring across the quilt center, including the borders just added in the measurement. Cut the top and bottom inner bor-ders this length. Stitch the top and bottom inner borders to the quilt center, pinning to match centers and ends, easing where necessary to fit. Press the seams toward the borders.

Outer Border
Sew together 1 ½" x 5" strips into pairs, and join pairs into panels of 4. Press seams to one side. Join units side-by-side arranging scrap colors in a pleasing manner. You will need about 280" of piano key border.

B If you are strip piecing, piece the 1 ½" scraps into panels of 4 strips each. Sub-cut into 5" units as shown in the diagram. Join the units side-by-side arranging the colors in a pleasing manner. You will need about 280" of piano key border.

Border Corners
C Though the quilt looks like it has mitered corners, it doesn't! If you are using the Easy Angle Ruler, place 2 lengths of border with right sides facing. Using the Easy Angle Ruler, cut 4 triangle pairs using the 5" line

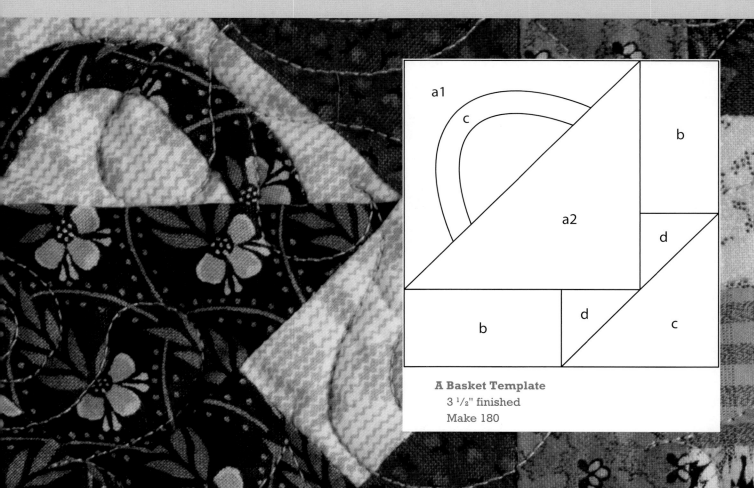

A Basket Template
3 ½" finished
Make 180

on the ruler. Stitch. Press. Corner units will measure 5" unfinished, the same width as your border.

Note: There is sufficient length in the piano key border if you use the Easy Angle Ruler.

D If you are sewing without the Easy Angle Ruler, cut about 24-26 random strips 1 ½" x 6". Join them side by side to make a length measuring approximately 24" long. Press. Cut into 4 – 6" squares.

Place the squares right sides together with stripes facing the same direction. Slice on the diagonal to yield 4 triangle pairs. Stitch pairs into 4 corner units. Trim to 5" square.

Note: The strips are not intended to meet at the center seam to add variety and character!

Lay out the quilt top and measure from top to bottom through the center including the border just added. Cut 2 side borders from the piano key border this length.

Measure side to side through the quilt center including the gold inner border and cut a top and bottom border this length.

Add the side borders to the quilt center, pinning to match centers and ends. Stitch. Press to the inner gold borders. Add the mitered corner squares to each end of the top and bottom borders and stitch these to the quilt center, pinning to match centers and ends. Press to the inner borders.

After the borders are added, set your machine to a bit longer stitch length, and stay stitch around the outside edge of the quilt top to prevent any seams from opening as the quilt is handled in the quilting process.

FINISHING

Lucy's Baskets is quilted in gold thread in an edge-to-edge design called Holly's Hearts by Patricia Ritter of Urban Elementz. Refer to the resources page for contact information.

The quilt is finished with a deep wine print for the binding.

AT A GLANCE

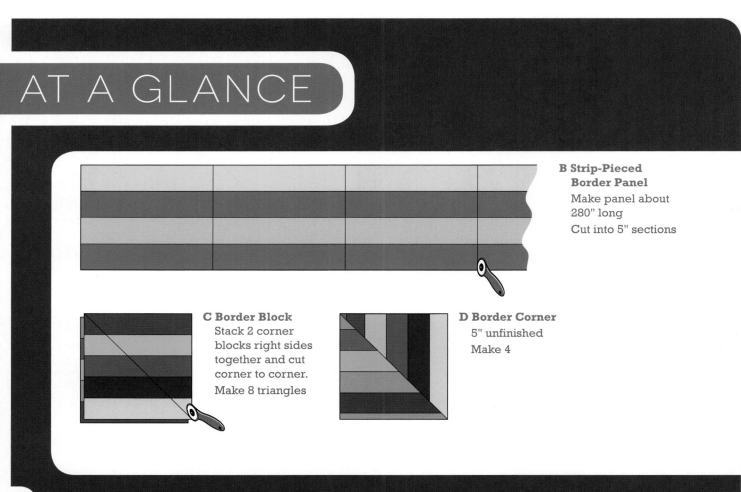

B Strip-Pieced Border Panel
Make panel about 280" long
Cut into 5" sections

C Border Block
Stack 2 corner blocks right sides together and cut corner to corner.
Make 8 triangles

D Border Corner
5" unfinished
Make 4

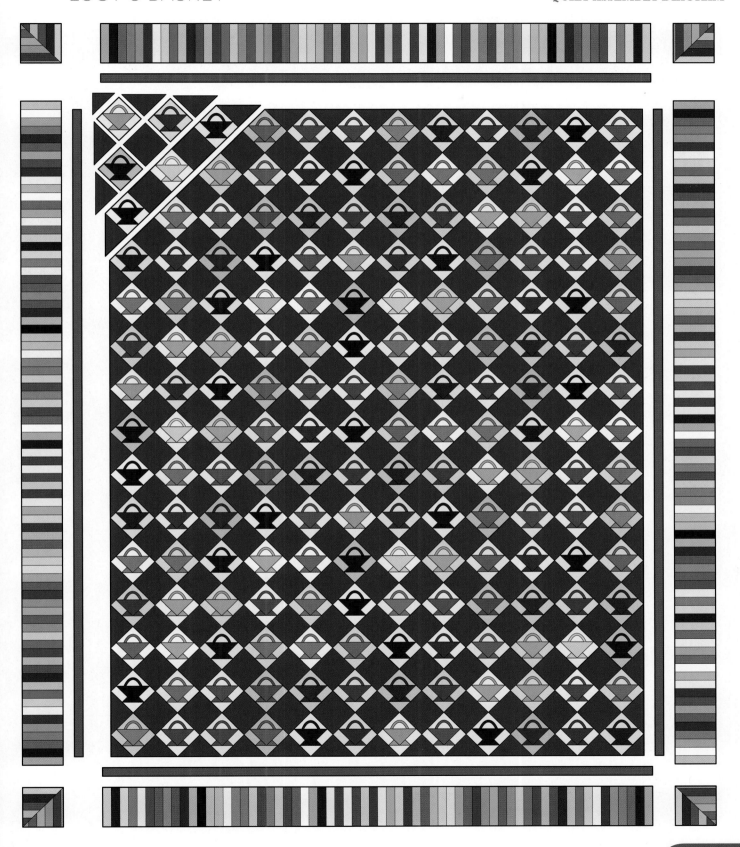

CHEDDAR BOWTIES

QUILT STATISTICS
MADE BY BONNIE K. HUNTER
SIZE 90" X 90"
BLOCKS: 729 – 3" FINISHED
PIECED BORDER: 4 ¹/₂" FINISHED

It's been fun to watch the Leaders and Enders phenomenon take the quilting world by storm! It's easy to make four-patches or nine-patches – but what if we set out to make a particular quilt using Leader and Ender units over the course of a year? That's what happened with this quilt.

July 2011 found me at the Sisters Quilt Show in Sisters, Ore., with a group of friends – all of us enamored by a certain bowtie quilt on a bright cheddar background. We could make this! But there were hundreds of bowties - how about we do this as a Leader and Ender project? The challenge was born!

Over the course of the year the instructions were to cut pieces from scraps, set them by your machine, and as you are sewing on regular projects – use the bow-tie pieces as Leaders and Enders just to see how many could be made in a year. How many did I make in a year? 729!

FABRICS

Blocks and Border

- 4 ¹/₂ yards of cheddar
- 7 ¾ yards total of light and dark scraps

Binding

- ³/₄ yard of dark brown print

CUTTING

Blocks

From the scraps, cut:
- 2 – 2" squares per block
- 2 – 1 ¼" connector squares per block

Tip: I found it easy to cut the main bowtie pieces out of a 2" x 6 ½" strip, which helped me use the smallest of scraps.

- From the cheddar, cut 2 – 2" squares per block, 1,458 total

Border

- From the light and dark scraps, cut 684 – 2" squares

Binding

- From the dark brown, cut 10 – 2 ½" x the width of fabric strips

Diagrams are on page 40-41.

PIECING

Connector Units

A Place a 1 ¼" connector square in the corner of a cheddar background square with right-sides together. Sew on the diagonal from corner to corner. Fold the corner up to be sure the edges meet where you wish. Trim excess fabric ¼" from the stitching line and press. Make 2 connector units for each block.

Blocks

B Position 2 connector units and 2 bowtie squares as shown in the diagram. Stitch into rows, and join rows to complete the block. Press. Make 729 blocks.

Quilt Top Center Assembly

Lay out the blocks in 27 rows of 27 blocks across. Join the blocks into rows and join the rows to complete the quilt top center. Press.

Checkerboard Border

This border could also be pieced as Leaders and Enders from 2" cut squares. But if you are in a hurry you can strip piece it. Join lengths of 2" wide scrap strips into sets of 3. I didn't pay attention to light or dark, I just sewed them randomly.

How many strip sets you need depends on how long your strips are. What matters more is how many sub-cuts you need from your strip sets. For this quilt you need 228 – 2" sub-cuts.

C Join the 2" sub-cut sections together to make 4 borders, 54 sections long. Press. Set the 12 remaining sub-cut sections aside.

Border Corners

D Using the remaining 12 sub-cut sections from above, join 3 sections together to make 1 nine-patch border corner. Make 4. Press.

Add the side checkerboard borders to the quilt, pinning to match centers and ends, easing where necessary to fit. Press seam toward the border just added.

Add the nine-patch corner bocks to each end of the top and bottom borders. Join the top and bottom borders to the quilt, pinning as above. Press the seams toward the borders just added.

Stay stitch slightly less than $1/4$" from the edge of the quilt top to keep the checkerboard border seams from popping open. It will be covered by binding after quilting.

FINISHING

Cheddar Bowties was quilted in an antique tan colored thread in an edge-to-edge spider web design called Entangled by Gali Design. Refer to the resources page for contact information.

The quilt is finished with a dark chocolate brown binding.

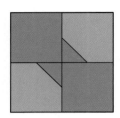

A Connector Units
2" unfinished
Make 2 per block

B Bowtie Block
3" finished
Make 729

C Checkerboard Border
4 1/2" x 81" finished
Make 4

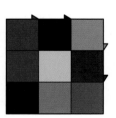

D Border Corner
4 1/2" finished
Make 4

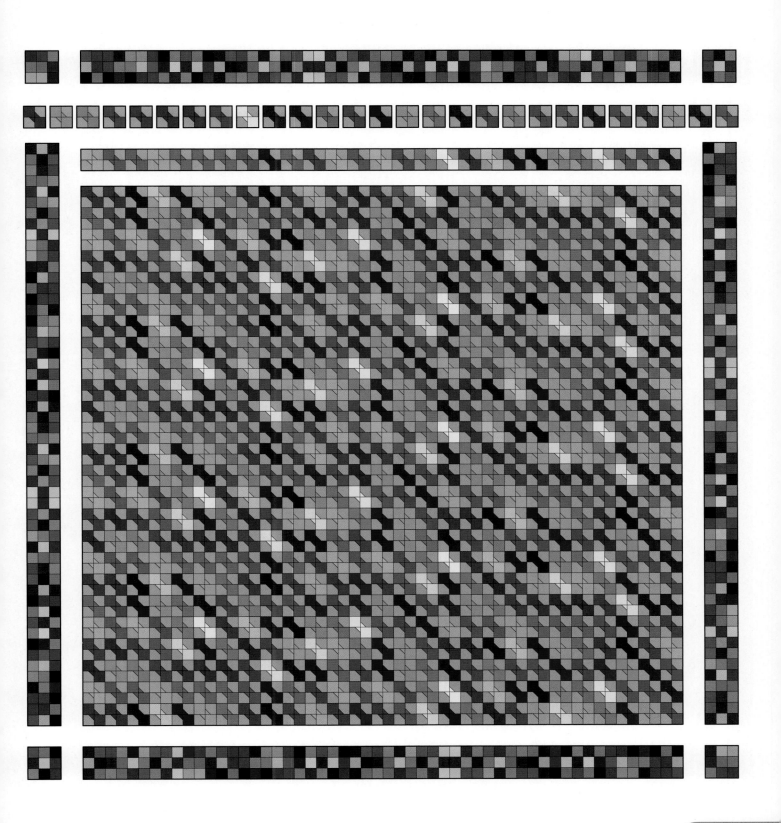

FOUR-PATCH X

QUILT STATISTICS
MADE BY BONNIE K. HUNTER
SIZE 73 ³/₄" X 83 ¹/₂"
BLOCKS: 56 – 8 ¹/₄" FINISHED
SASHING: 1 ¹/₂" WIDE FINISHED
PIECED OUTER BORDER: 2" WIDE FINISHED

Always on the lookout for ways to use Leader and Ender four patches, this traditional design – known as Sarah's Favorite by Ladies Art Company – called to me. I love blocks with strong diagonals, and this has them going in both directions. And what if we created a secondary design with the sashing and cornerstones and pump up the look of a churn dash where they all come together? Even more fun!

No special attention was paid to the direction the four-patches are facing in these blocks. Some are light/dark variations and some are scrappy everything. There are even some that were left from other projects that are made with two fabrics only, instead of four. All find a place in this very fun and scrappy quilt.

FABRICS

Blocks and border

- 3 ¹/₂ yards of light and dark scraps
- 2 ¹/₂ yards of yellow solid
- 1 ¹/₂ yards of navy for blocks, cornerstones and the pieced border

Sashing and Borders

- 1 ¹/₂ yards of blue stripe
- ³/₄ yard of red scraps

Binding

- ³/₄ yard of navy

CUTTING

Four-Patch Units

- From the light and dark scraps, cut 1,120 – 2" squares

Blocks

- From the yellow, cut 56 – 5 ½" squares. Cut the squares twice on the diagonal with an X to yield 224 quarter-square triangles.
- From the navy print scraps, cut 112 – 3" squares. Cut each square corner to corner once on the diagonal to yield 4 corner triangles per block, 224 total.

Sashing

- From the blue stripe, cut 7 – 6 ¾" x the width of fabric. Make sure the stripe runs the length of the sashing. Sub-cut into 127 – 2" x 6 ¾" rectangles.

  Note: Measure your blocks before you cut the sashing rectangles. If your blocks are a different size, cut the rectangles 2" less than the length of your blocks.

- From the red scraps, cut 254 – 1 ½" x 2" rectangles
- From the navy, cut 72 – 2" squares for the cornerstones

Pieced Outer Border

- From the yellow, cut 30 – 2 ½" x 8 ¾" rectangles.

Note: Cut the yellow rectangles the same size as the sashing strips above, after the red rectangles have been added to each end if your block size is different. From the navy scraps, cut 60 – 2 ½" squares. Draw a line from corner to corner on the back of each one.

- From the red scraps, cut 34 – 1 ½" x 2" rectangles
- From the yellow, cut 34 – 1 ½" x 2" rectangles
- From the navy scraps, cut 2 – 2 ⅞" squares
- From the yellow, cut 2 – 2 ⅞" squares

Binding

- From the navy, cut 10 – 2 ½" x the width of fabric strips

Diagrams are on pages 46-47.

PIECING

Four-Patch Units

All of the four-patches in this quilt were constructed in the Leader and Ender method in between other sewing. Because I trim scraps down as I go, I already had a box of 2" squares on hand for easy piecing. When constructing the four patches, make sure to spin the seams as shown on page 12. This ensures that no matter what direction you turn them, the seams will always nest together.

A Stitch 2 pairs of squares together. Press to one side. Sew these units together to make the finished four-patch units. Make 280 four-patches. The units measure 3 ½" unfinished and will finish at 3".

As I made my four-patch units, I pinned them in bundles of 10 so it was easy for me to count how many I had. It's easier to keep track that way!

Note: If you choose to strip piece the blocks, cut the assorted scraps into 2" strips. Since the length of your scrap strips determines the number of units you can get from them, no exact number of strips to cut is given. Piece the scrap strips in pairs. Sub-cut into 560 – 2" units. Sew together to make 280 four-patch units.

Block Assembly

Each block is made of 5 four-patch units, 4 yellow side triangles and 4 navy corner triangles.

B-C The Four-Patch X block is sewn in diagonal rows. Lay out the block pieces as shown in the diagram on page 46. Stitch the units into rows and join the rows to complete each block. The blocks will measure 8 ¾" and finish at 8 ¼". Make 56.

Sashing

D Sew a red rectangle to each end of the striped sashing strips. Press the seams toward the red rectangles. The sashing strips will measure 8 ¾" long unfinished and finish at 8 ¼".

Quilt Top Center Assembly

Referring to the quilt assembly diagram on page 47, lay out the blocks in rows along with the sashing units and the navy cornerstones. Stitch the quilt center into rows, pressing the seams toward the sashing, and away from the cornerstones. Join the rows to complete the quilt center.

Borders

The final border completes the churn dashes around the outside of the quilt. This is done in 2 parts – with triangles added to the ends of the border sashing, and a spacer cornerstone made from a red and a yellow rectangle.

Border Sashing Unit

E-F Place a navy square, right-sides together, with the border rectangle at each end of the rectangle. Sew on each diagonal line, paying attention to which direction the diagonal line is facing. Trim the excess ¹/₄" beyond the stitching. Press the seams toward the triangles. Make 30.

Border Spacer Units

G Sew 1 red rectangle to 1 yellow rectangle. Press seams to the red. Units will measure 2" x 2 ¹/₂" unfinished and 1 ¹/₂" x 2" square finished. Make 34.

Border Corners

H Place the yellow squares, right-sides together, with the blue squares and cut once on the diagonal from corner to corner to yield 4 matched triangle pairs. Sew the pairs together on the bias edge to make 4 corner half-square triangles. Press to the dark. Units will measure 2 ¹/₂" square unfinished and will finish at 2".

Border Assembly

Side Borders

Join 8 border rectangles and 9 border cornerstones side by side into one border length, pressing seams toward the border cornerstone units. Make 2 side borders this length.

Sew the outer pieced borders to the quilt sides with right-sides together, pinning to match the seams. Ease where necessary to fit. Press seams toward the striped sashing.

Add a yellow/blue half square triangle corner unit to each end of the top and bottom border, paying attention to which way the triangles turn to complete each corner churn dash.

Top and Bottom Borders

Repeat the process above, alternating 8 cornerstone units with 7 pieced border units. Make 2.

Sew the outer pieced borders to the quilt sides with right sides together, pinning to match seams. Ease where necessary to fit. Press seams toward the striped sashing.

FINISHING

Four-Patch X is machine quilted with an edge-to-edge design called Espalier by Hermione Agee of Lorien Quilting, Austrailia. Refer to the resources page for contact information.

A starry navy binding was a great way to bring the navy from the churn dashes to the edge of the quilt.

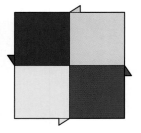

A Four-Patch Unit
3 ¹/₂" unfinished
Make 280

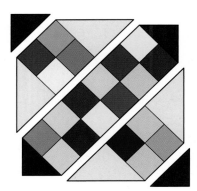

B Four-Patch X Block Construction

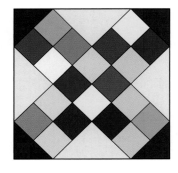

C Four-Patch X Block
8 ³/₄" unfinished
Make 56

D Pieced Sashing
2" x 8 ³/₄" unfinished
Make 127

E Border Sashing Construction
Flip and stitch navy square to the ends of the border sashing strip.

F Border Sashing Unit
2 ¹/₂" x 8 ³/₄" unfinished
Make 30

G Border Spacer Units
2" x 2 ¹/₂" square unfinished
Make 34

H 2 ¹/₂" square unfinished
Make 4

FOUR-PATCH X

TEXAS TUMBLEWEEDS

QUILT STATISTICS
MADE BY BONNIE K HUNTER
SIZE: 75" X 83"
LADDER BLOCK: 36 – 8" FINISHED
SPINNING STAR BLOCK: 36 – 8" FINISHED
INNER BORDER: 1" FINISHED
OUTER BORDER: 4 ¹/₂"

An invitation to teach a mystery quilt over New Year's Eve in Plano, Tex., at Fabric Fanatics had me scrambling for the batiks I'd always wanted to dig into. Fabric Fanatics specializes in batik fabrics, and I wanted my quilt to fit the theme!

A combination of two different blocks, a symmetrical spinning star and an asymmetrical ladder block, give this quilt two different eye-catching diagonals. Even better, the blocks are made completely from 2 ¹/₂" wide strips, making it easy to dig into your pre-cut strip stash and sew away.

While assembling my star blocks, I thought ahead and cut 2 ¹/₂" squares of both the dark brown and neutral fabric for the four patches found in the center of the ladder blocks. Yep! You guessed it! The center four patches were my Leaders and Enders during the construction of this quilt.

FABRICS

Blocks

- 2 ³/₄ yards of assorted medium to dark colored batik, tone-on-tone and print scraps for the star blocks
- 1 ¹/₂ yards of brown, tone-on-tone and print scraps for the ladder blocks
- 4 yards of assorted neutral batiks, tone on tone and print scraps for both block backgrounds

Borders

- ¹/₂ yard of raspberry batik for the inner border
- 1 ¹/₂ yards of green batik for the outer border

Binding

- ³/₄ yard of purple batik

CUTTING

Ladder Block

Four-Patch Units
- From the brown, cut 72 – 2 ¹/₂" squares
- From the neutrals, cut 72 – 2 ¹/₂" squares

Rectangle Units

- From the brown, cut:
  144 – 2 ¹/₂" squares for corner triangles
  72 – 2 ¹/₂" squares for block corners
- From the neutrals, cut:
  144 – 2 ¹/₂" x 4 ¹/₂" rectangles
  72 – 2 ¹/₂" squares for block corners

Spinning Star Block

Unit 1
- From medium to dark colored scraps, cut 144 – 2 ¹/₂" x 4 ¹/₂" rectangles
- From neutral scraps, cut 144 – 2 ¹/₂" squares

Unit 2
- From the medium to dark colored scraps, cut 288 – 2 ¹/₂" squares
- From the neutral scraps, cut 144 – 2 ¹/₂" x 4 ¹/₂" rectangles

Borders

- From the raspberry, cut 8 – 1 ¹/₂" x the width of fabric strips for the inner borders
- From the green, cut 9 – 5" x the width of fabric strips for the outer borders

Binding

- From the purple, cut 9 – 2 ¹/₂" x the width of fabric strips

Diagrams are on page 52-53.

PIECING

Ladder Block

Four-Patch Units
You can make your four patches Leader and Ender style or use the strip piecing method found on page 13.

Four patch construction
A Using 2 – 2 ¹/₂" brown squares and 2 – 2 ¹/₂" neutral squares, make a four-patch unit as shown in the diagram. Repeat to make 36 – 4 ¹/₂" unfinished units for the ladder blocks.

Rectangle Units
B The ladder block requires 2 rectangle units with right-hand corner triangles and 2 rectangle units with left-hand corner triangles in mirror image of each other.

Draw a line from corner to corner on the back of the brown squares. Place a brown square on top of a neutral rectangle on one end. Stitch on the line from corner to corner. Press the square back along the stitching line over to the corner of the rectangle to be sure that the edges of the square align with the edges of the rectangle. Trim the excess beyond the ¹/₄" seam allowance and press toward the dark fabric.

Stitch 72 units with the corner pointing to the right, and 72 with the corner pointing to the left! Press seams toward the dark corners just added. Units will measure 2 ¹/₂" x 4 ¹/₂" unfinished and finish at 2" x 4".

Ladder Block Assembly
D-E The ladder block is made of 1 four-patch unit, 2 brown squares, 2 neutral squares and 4 rectangle units. Lay out the units as shown in the diagram. Pay attention to which direction the brown squares chain across the ladder. Join units into rows and join the rows to complete the block. Make 36 blocks. Blocks measure 8 ¹/₂" square unfinished and finish at 8".

Spinning Star Block

Unit 1
F Draw a line from corner to corner on the back of the neutral squares. Place a neutral square on top of a colored rectangle. Stitch on the line from corner to corner. Press the square back along the stitching line over to the corner of the rectangle to be sure that the edges of the square align with the edges of the rectangle. Trim the excess beyond the ¹/₄" seam allowance and press the seams toward the neutral triangle.

Make 144. Units will measure 2 ¹/₂" x 4 ¹/₂" and finish at 2" x 4".

Unit 2
G Draw a line from corner to corner on the back of the colored squares. Place a colored square on the top and at one end of a neutral rectangle. Following the diagram, be sure seams are angled correctly. Stitch on the line from corner to corner. Press the square back along the stitching line over to the corner of the rectangle to be sure that the edge of the square

aligns with the edges of the rectangle. Trim the excess beyond the 1/4" seam allowance and press the seams toward the colored triangle. Repeat on the other end of the rectangle. Units will measure 2 1/2" x 4 1/2" and finish at 2" x 4".

Note: The seams for Unit 2 angle in the opposite direction of Unit 1.

Spinning Star Unit

H Sew a Unit 1 to a Unit 2 as shown in the diagram on page 50. Press seam toward Unit 1. Make 144 quarter units. Each will measure 4 1/2" square and finish at 4".

Spinning Star Assembly

I Arrange 4 block quarters as shown in the diagram and join to complete one spinning star block. Make 36. The block will measure 8 1/2" square and finish at 8".

Quilt Top Center Assembly

Layout the blocks in 9 rows of 8 blocks, alternating spinning star and ladder blocks as shown in the quilt assembly diagram on page 53. Join blocks into rows and join rows to complete quilt center. Press.

Borders

Inner Border

Join the 8 border strips end-to-end with diagonal seams to make a strip approximately 320" long. Trim the excess beyond the 1/4" seam allowance and press the seams open.

Lay the quilt center out on the floor, smoothing it gently. Do not tug or pull. Measure the quilt through the center from top to bottom. Cut two inner side borders to this length. Sew the inner side borders to the quilt sides with right sides together, pinning to match centers and ends. Ease where necessary to fit. Press the seams toward the borders.

Repeat for the top and bottom inner borders, measuring across the quilt center, including the borders just added in the measurement. Cut the top and bottom inner borders this length. Stitch the top and bottom inner borders to the quilt center, pinning to match centers and ends, easing where necessary to fit. Press the seams toward the borders.

Outer Border

Join the 9 border strips end to end on the straight of grain to make a strip approximately 360" long. Press seams open. Add the outer borders in the same manner as the inner borders were added.

FINISHING

Texas Tumbleweeds was machine quilted in antique gold thread with an edge to edge design called Damask Feathers by Hermoine Agee of Lorien Quilting, Australia. Refer to the resources page for contact information.

A purple batik binding finishes the edge, picking up one of the colors in the border fabric.

AT A GLANCE

A Four Patch Units
4 ¹/₂" square unfinished
Make 36

B Rectangle Unit Construction

C Rectangle Units
2 ¹/₂" x 4 ¹/₂" unfinished
Make 72 each

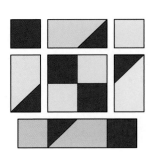

D Ladder Block Assembly

E Ladder Block
8 ¹/₂" square unfinished
Make 36

F Spinning Star Unit 1
2 ¹/₂" x 4 ¹/₂" unfinished
Make 144

G Spinning Star Unit 2
2 ¹/₂" x 4 ¹/₂" unfinished
Make 144

H Spinning Star Quarter Unit
4 ¹/₂" square
Make 144

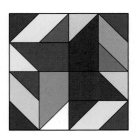

I Spinning Star Block
8 ¹/₂" square unfinished
Make 36

SPOOLIN' AROUND

QUILT STATISTICS
MADE BY BONNIE K. HUNTER
SIZE: 89 ¹/₂" X 98"
BLOCKS: 162 – 6" SQUARE FINISHED
INNER BORDERS: ³/₄" WIDE FINISHED
PIECED OUTER BORDER: 4 ¹/₄" WIDE FINISHED

Every year on my blog, I issue a Leader and Ender challenge for readers to sew throughout the year. Many quilters have found themselves swapping strips and block parts to build up the variety in their quilts. It was fun to include other people's scraps with mine! Every scrap that hit my cutting table during this time was cut into spool pieces as part of the clean-up process. There is everything in this quilt – Halloween, vintage Christmas, old calicoes, Civil War reproductions, solids, recycled plaids and stripes, batiks and novelties. They all tell the story of the fabric that has come through my hands as a quilter!

The border is also Leader and Ender generated – after making several quilts for this book with the ever-stockpiled four-patches on hand, I still had enough to piece into this border. Leaders and Enders are the quilter's gift that keeps on giving.

FABRICS

Blocks

- 5 ¹/₃ yards total of neutral scraps for the backgrounds and pieced outer border
- 7 ¹/₂ yards total of medium to dark colored scraps for blocks and pieced outer borders

Setting/Corner Triangles

- 1 ¹/₄ yards of fuchsia pink for the setting triangles

Borders

- ³/₄ yard of white with pink stripe for the inner borders 1 and 3
- ³/₈ yard of black print for inner border 2
- 1 ¹/₂ yards of green print for pieced outer border triangles

Binding

- 1 yard of fuschia pink

CUTTING

For 1 Spool Unit

- From the neutral scraps, cut 2 – 1 ¹/₂" x 3 ¹/₂" rectangles

From the colored scraps, cut:

- 1 – 1 ¹/₂" x 3 ¹/₂" rectangle
- 4 – 1 ¹/₂" squares

Setting/Corner Triangles

- From the fuschia pink, cut 9 – 9 ³/₄" squares. Cut each square twice on the diagonal with an X to yield 36 quarter-square setting triangles. You need 34 to set the quilt, and there will be 2 left over.

- From the fuchsia pink, cut 2 – 5 $\frac{1}{8}$" squares. Cut each square once on the diagonal from corner to corner to yield 4 corner triangles.

Borders

Inner Borders
- From white and pink stripe cut, 18 – 1 $\frac{1}{4}$" x the width of the fabric strips
- From black print cut, 9 – 1 $\frac{1}{4}$" x the width of the fabric strips

Outer Borders
- From the light, medium and dark scraps, cut 336 – 2" squares
- From the green fabric, cut 40 – 5 $\frac{1}{2}$" squares. Cut each square twice on the diagonal with an X to yield 160 side triangles.
- From the green fabric, cut 2 – 5 $\frac{1}{8}$" squares. Cut squares once on the diagonal to yield 4 corner triangles.

Binding
- From the fuschia pink, cut 11 – 2 $\frac{1}{2}$" x the width of fabric strips.

Diagrams are on page 60-61.

PIECING

Don't faint! This quilt contains 648 individual spools! That is less than two spools per day over the course of a year. You can do this! I found that it helped me to know that I didn't have to cut out the whole quilt at once, just cut enough at a time to sew some. And when I needed more, I cut some more.

A Draw a diagonal line on the back of each of the 4 colored squares. Place a square on either end of the spool background rectangle with right sides together. Stitch on the diagonal, and flip the triangle back to be sure it meets the edges of the rectangle. Trim the excess beyond the $\frac{1}{4}$" seam allowance and press the seams open. Make 2.

B Sew a colored rectangle between the 2 spool end rectangles and stitch. Press seams toward the center rectangle. The spool unit measures 3 $\frac{1}{2}$" square and finishes at 3". Make 648 spool units.

Block Assembly

Lay out 4 spool units as shown in the diagram to make one Spoolin' Around block. Join the units into rows and join the rows to complete the block. Be sure to spin the seams as shown on page 12. Make 162 blocks.

Quilt Top Center Assembly

Spoolin' Around is an on-point setting, assembled in diagonal rows. Referring to the quilt assembly diagram on page 61, lay out the blocks in diagonal rows adding the setting triangles and corner triangles to the ends of the rows. I like to piece on-point quilts into 2 halves. This keeps things from being too unwieldy, especially when sewing a large quilt top. Join the quilt top halves to complete quilt center. Press.

After piecing the top center, trim the seam allowance $\frac{1}{4}$" from the block corners, using a ruler with a $\frac{1}{4}$" marking. This removes dog ears and makes sure the top is square before adding the borders.

Borders

Inner Borders
Three narrow inner borders are joined with butted seams one at a time to float the quilt center and to have the math work with the pieced outer border.

Join the 18 white and pink stripe border strips end to end with diagonal seams to make a strip approximately 720" long. Trim the excess $\frac{1}{4}$" from the seams and press open.

Join the 9 black border strips end to end with diagonal seams to make a strip approximately 360" long. Trim the excess $\frac{1}{4}$" from the seams and press open.

Lay the quilt center out on the floor, smoothing it gently. Do not tug or pull. Measure the quilt through the center from top to bottom. Cut 2 inner side borders this length from the white and pink stripe fabric. Sew the inner side borders to the quilt sides with right sides together, pinning to match centers and ends. Ease where necessary to fit. Press the seams toward the borders.

Repeat for top and bottom inner borders, measuring across the quilt center, including the borders just added in the measurement. Cut the top and bottom inner borders to this length. Stitch the top and bottom inner borders to the quilt center, pinning to match centers and ends, easing where necessary to fit. Press seams toward the borders.

Repeat twice more, next with the black border strip, and finally again with the remaining white and pink border strip. Be careful not to tug or pull – it is important to keep this accurate so the outer pieced border will fit.

Pieced Outer Borders

Four-Patch Units
You can make your four patches Leader and Ender style or use the strip piecing method found on page 13.

D Using 4 of the light, medium and dark 2" squares make a four-patch unit as shown in the diagram. Repeat to make 84 – 3 ½" units.

E Join 2 side triangles with 1 four patch as shown in the diagram, Press the seams toward the side triangles. Make 72 border units.

F Join 2 side triangles to one border four patch as shown in the diagram. Press the seams toward the side triangles. Make 4 border end units.

G Join 2 four patches side by side. Press. Add a side triangle to each end as shown in the diagram on page 58. Press the seams toward the side triangles. Stitch a corner triangle to the unit, pressing seams toward the corner triangle. Make 4 border corner units.

Border Assembly
Referring to the quilt assembly diagram on page 61, join 19 border units end to end in one long length. Press. Make 2 side borders. Join 17 border units end to end in one long length. Press. Make 2 top and bottom borders.

Add a border end unit to the right end of each of the four borders. Ends should give a trapezoidal appearance as

shown. The top and bottom borders will now have 18 four patches, and the longer side borders should have a total of 20 four patches each.

Using your rotary cutter and the ¼" line on your ruler, true up the edges of the borders ¼" from the corner of each four patch on both long sides of each border to eliminate dog ears and any bowing.

Join the side borders to the quilt sides, matching centers and extending the pointed border ends ¼" beyond the edge of the inner borders – these are the dog ears. Ease where necessary to fit. Press the seams toward the inner borders.

Add the top and bottom borders to the quilt in the same way, pinning to match centers and ends, extending the ends ¼" beyond the edge of the inner border and overlapping the ends of the side borders, easing where necessary to fit. Press the seams toward the inner borders.

Sew a corner unit to each corner of the quilt to complete the pieced border surrounding the quilt. Because the dog ears were overlapped when joining the borders to the quilt, there should be ¼" depth of seam allowance at each corner of the inner border to prevent the loss of the corner within the seam. Press.

FINISHING

Spoolin' Around was machine quilted in antique gold thread with an edge-to-edge design called Amorphous by Hermoine Agee of Lorien Quilting, Australia. Refer to the resources page for contact information.

The quilt was bound in the same fuschia pink as the center setting triangles.

On the Flip Side

Don't forget the backside! I cleared out a whole boat-load of old dusty rose and mauve pinks from the 1980s-1990s stash that needed a place to go. I also attacked the orphan box, including gifted blocks and anything that had pink in it to help add some interest. The back is almost – ALMOST – as fun as the front!

A Spool Background Rectangle
1 ¹/₂" x 3 ¹/₂" unfinished
Make 2 per block

B Spool Unit
3 ¹/₂" square
unfinished
Make 648

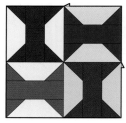

C Spoolin' Around Block
6 ¹/₂" unfinished
Make 162

D Four Patch Units
3 ¹/₂" square unfinished
Make 84

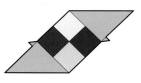

E Border Unit
Make 72

F-Border End Unit
Make 4

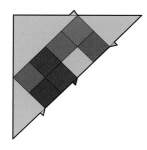

G-Border Corner Unit
Make 4

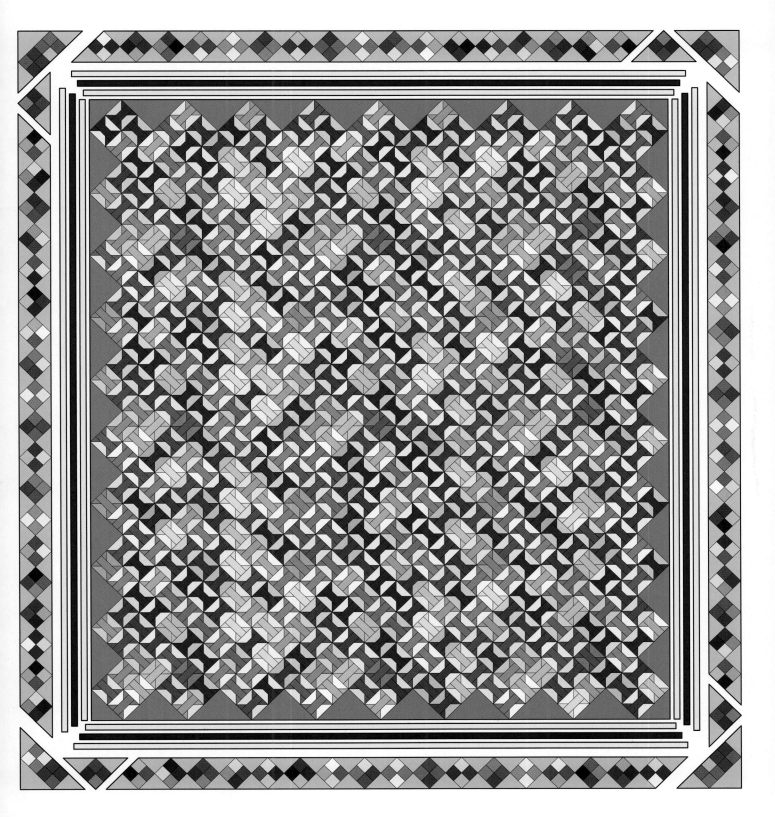

QUILT STATISTICS
MADE BY BONNIE K. HUNTER
SIZE: 81" X 87"
BLOCKS: 287 – 3" FINISHED
INNER BORDER: 1½" WIDE FINISHED
OUTER BORDER: 4½" WIDE FINISHED

In Spring 2012, I visited the Ninigret Quilters of Rhode Island and spent a bit of time exploring the local beauty around Narragansett Bay. In October 2012, I was mourning the devastation that befell beautiful Narragansett in the aftermath of Hurricane Sandy.

As the hurricane raged, I sewed and sewed. Finally, I ended up with this quilt. I entitled it simply Narragansett Blues. The blue matched my mood – the blue in the morning sky brings hope in the new day.

Lesson learned? Always keep a good supply of Leader and Ender four-patches on hand – you never know when a project demands to be made while storms rise and rage!

FABRICS

Blocks

- 2 ½ yards of neutral scraps for the blocks and pieced outer border
- 2 ¾ yards of medium to dark scraps for the blocks and pieced outer border
- 2 ½ yards of blue scraps for the bricks and squares

Borders

- ½ yard of red for the inner border
- ³/₈ yard of red scraps for the pieced outer border

Binding

- ¾ yard navy

CUTTING

Four-Patch Units

- From the neutral scraps, cut 574 – 2" squares
- From the medium to dark scraps, cut 574 – 2" squares

Bricks and Squares

- From the assorted blue scraps, cut 126 – 3 ½" x 6 ½" rectangles
- From the assorted blue scraps, cut 36 – 3 ½" squares

BORDERS

Inner border

- From the red print, cut 8 – 2" x the width of fabric strips

Outer border

- From neutral scraps, cut 200 – 2" squares
- From dark to medium scraps, cut 300 – 2" squares
- From the red scraps, cut 104 – 2" squares
- From random scraps, cut 32 – 2" squares for the border corners

Binding

- From the navy, cut 10 – 2 ½" x the width of fabric strips

Diagrams are on pages 66-67.

PIECING

Four-Patch Units

All of the 287 four-patches for this quilt were made as Leaders and Enders while I was assembling other quilts. You can make your four-patches Leader and Ender style or use the strip piecing method found on page 13. When constructing the four-patches, make sure to spin the seams as shown on page 12. This ensures that no matter what direction you turn them, the seams will always nest together.

Four patch construction

A Stitch a light and a dark square with right sides together. Press to one side. Make 574 light/dark pairs. Sew these units together to make the finished four-patch units. Make 287. The units measure 3 ½" unfinished and will finish at 3".

As I made my four-patch units, I pinned them in bundles of 10 so it was easy for me to count how many I had.

Note: If you choose to strip piece the blocks, cut the assorted scraps into 2" strips. Since the length of your scrap strips determines the number of units you can get from them, no exact number of strips to cut is given. Working with short strips helps increase your variety. Piece the scrap strips in pairs. Sub-cut into 574– 2" units. Sew together to make 287 four-patch blocks.

Quilt Top Center Assembly

Narragansett Blues is most easily constructed in vertical rows. Single and double units of the four-patches are sewn in between the bricks. The squares are used as fillers for the ends of the rows where a single brick is too long. They are also used around the single center four-patch.

Referring to the quilt assembly diagram on page 67, join the bricks, four-patches and squares into long vertical rows the length of the quilt. Press seams toward the bricks and squares as much as possible. Join the rows to complete the quilt top center. Press.

BORDERS

Inner Border

Join the 8 red inner border strips end to end on the diagonal to make a strip approximately 320" long. Press the seams open.

Lay out the quilt center on the floor, smoothing it gently. Do not tug or pull. Measure the quilt through the center from top to bottom. Cut inner side borders this length. Sew the side borders to the quilt sides with right sides together, pinning to match centers and ends. Ease where necessary to fit. Press the seams toward the borders.

Repeat for the top and bottom borders, measuring across the quilt center, including the borders just added in the measurement. Cut the top and bottom borders this length. Stitch the top and bottom borders to the quilt center, pinning to match centers and ends, easing where necessary to fit. Press the seams toward the borders.

Outer Border

The outer border can easily be made as a Leader and Ender project as well, but it is likely that you are anxious to get the border done by the time you get the center pieced!

B Sew 100 sets of light/dark/light Unit A sets.
C Sew 100 sets of dark/red/dark Unit B sets.

Note: If you choose to strip piece the border units, cut the assorted scraps into short 2" strips. Short strips help build variety. Since the length of your scrap strips determines the number of units you can get from them, no exact number of strips to cut is given. Piece the scrap strips in sets of three: light/dark/light and dark/red/dark. Sub-cut into 2" units. Make 100 light/dark/light unit A's and 100 dark/red/dark unit B's.

Border Assembly

D Join 26 of Unit A and 26 of Unit B side by side creating a side border 52 units long. Make 2 borders this length, pressing seams in one direction. Sew the side borders to the quilt sides with right sides together, pinning to match centers and ends. Ease where necessary to fit. Press the seams toward the inner borders.

Join 24 of Unit A and 24 of Unit B side by side creating a top border 48 units long. Repeat for bottom border. Press.

E Randomly assemble the border corners scrap squares into 4 nine-patches all with red centers. Add a scrappy nine-patch to each end of the top and bottom borders. Press seams toward the nine-patches.

Sew the top and bottom borders to the quilt sides with right sides together, pinning to match centers and ends. Ease where necessary to fit. Press the seams toward the borders.

Note: This border is made with an even number of units. There may be a couple of places where two dark squares come together to interrupt the red/dark/red of the center row of the pieced border as it meets the nine-patch cornerstone. Let it go! It is the way it is – scrap happy!

FINISHING

Narragansett Blues was quilted using a blue-gray thread in an edge to edge design called Amorphous by Hermione Agee of Lorien Quilting, Australia. Refer to the resources page for contact information.

A dark navy blue binding brings the restful range of blues from the quilt center to the edge of the quilt to finish.

AT A GLANCE

A Four-Patch Units
3 ¹/₂" square unfinished
Make 287

 B Border Unit A
Make 100

 C Border Unit B
Make 100

D Border Construction
Make 2 borders with 52 alternating A and B Units
Make 2 borders with 48 alternating A and B Units

E Nine-Patch Cornerstones
3 ¹/₂" square unfinished
Make 4

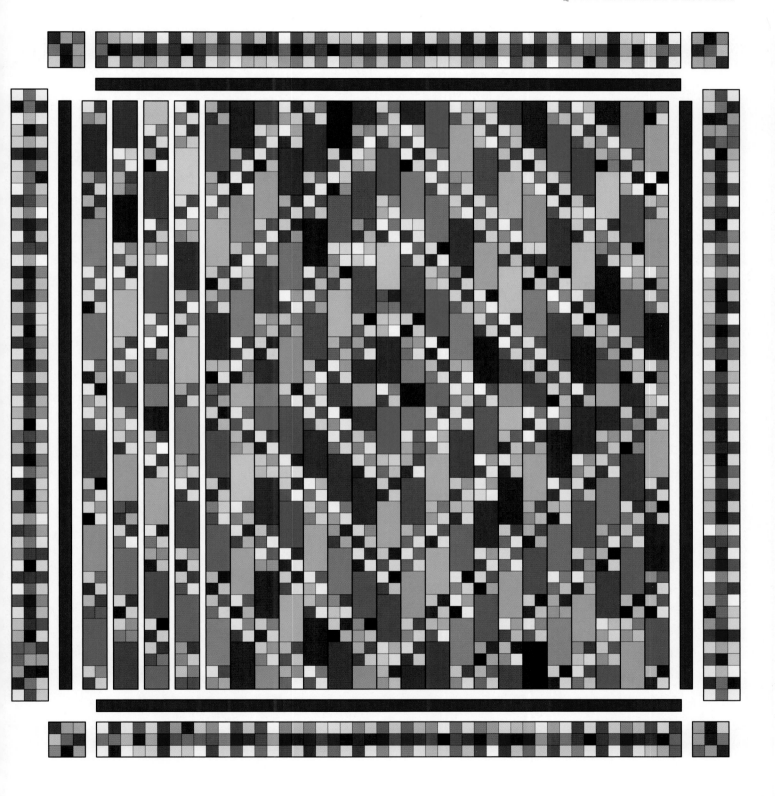

WINSTON WAYS

QUILT STATISTICS
MADE BY BONNIE K. HUNTER
SIZE: 74" X 86"
BLOCKS: 30 – 12" SQUARE FINISHED
INNER BORDER: 1" WIDE FINISHED
CHECKERBOARD BORDER: 2" WIDE FINISHED
OUTER BORDER: 4" WIDE FINISHED

I love to name quilts after places I've traveled through while working on them, and this one just had to be named for my adopted home town of Winston Salem, N.C.

I also love blocks that combine to create a secondary design, and the corner checkerboards of each block in this quilt meet giving the appearance of a two-block quilt set on point, when it is just one block set side by side. Don't faint – but get excited – there are 104 pieces in each 12" block!

I dug through my scraps choosing scrappy reds and neutrals for the checkerboard areas, blues – from aqua to navy and everywhere in between – for the star points. I used a wide range of neutrals, including stripes and plaids, for the star backgrounds and many different blacks and yellow/gold for the half-square triangles that surround each star.

FABRICS

Blocks

- 2 1/8 yards total of red scraps
- 3 yards total of neutral prints – white, cream and beige backgrounds
- 1 1/4 yards total of yellow to gold scraps
- 1 1/4 yards total of black scraps
- 1 yard total of assorted blue scraps from turquoise to navy

Borders

- 1/2 yard black print
- 1 1/4 yards blue print

Binding

- 3/4 yard of red scraps to make about 360" of binding

CUTTING

Four-Patch Units

- From the red scraps, cut 1,240 – 1 $\frac{1}{2}$" squares
- From the neutral scraps, cut 1,240 – 1 $\frac{1}{2}$" squares

Half-Square Triangle Units

- From the blue and neutral scraps, cut 30 sets of 4 matching - 2 $\frac{7}{8}$" squares
- From the black and gold scraps, cut 30 sets of 6 matching - 2 $\frac{7}{8}$" squares

If using the Easy Angle Ruler, cut blue 2 $\frac{1}{2}$" strips and neutral 2 $\frac{1}{2}$" strips.

Border

- From the black print, cut 8 – 1 $\frac{1}{2}$" x the width of fabric strips
- From the blue print, cut 8 – 4 $\frac{1}{2}$" x the width of fabric strips

Binding

- From the red scraps, cut 9 - 2 $\frac{1}{2}$" x the width of fabric strips

Diagrams are on page 73.

PIECING

Four-Patch Units

All of the 620 four-patches for this quilt were made as Leaders and Enders while I was assembling the other block parts. You can make your four-patches Leader and Ender style or use the strip piecing method found on page 13. When constructing the four-patches, make sure to spin the seams as shown on page 12 . This ensures that no matter what direction you turn them, the seams will always nest together.

Four-patch construction

A Using 2 – 1 ½" red print squares and 2 – 1 ½" neutral squares, make a four-patch unit as shown in the diagram. Be sure to spin the seams. Repeat to make 620 – 2 ½" units, unfinished – 480 for the blocks and 140 for the checkerboard border.

Half-Square Triangle Units

Blue/Neutral

B Layer the sets of blue and neutral squares with right sides together. Cut from corner to corner once on the diagonal to make 8 matched pairs. Stitch into 8 half-square triangle units, enough for 1 block. Press the seams toward the blue fabric and trim the dog ears. Make 30 sets.

If using the Easy Angle Ruler, match a blue and neutral strip with right sides together. Using the 2 ½" line on the ruler, cut the fabric into 240 matched pairs. Stitch the pairs together along the bias edge and press to the blue. The units should measure 2 ½" and finish at 2".

Gold/Black

C Layer the sets of black and gold squares with right sides together. Cut from corner to corner once on the diagonal to yield 8 matched pairs. Stitch into 8 half-square triangle units, enough for 1 block. Press the seams toward the black fabric and trim the dog ears. Make 30 sets.

Block Construction

Each block consists of 16 four-patch units, 12 black/gold half-square triangle units and 8 blue/neutral half-square triangle units.

D Paying attention to the direction the four-patches face, lay out 6 rows of 6 units each. Stitch the units into rows and join rows to complete each block, as shown in the diagram. Press each row in opposite directions so they nest when joined together. Make 30.

Quilt Top Center Assembly

Referring to the quilt assembly diagram on page 73, lay out the blocks in 6 rows of 5 blocks each. Join the blocks into rows and join the rows to complete quilt center. Press.

Borders

Inner Border

Join the 8 black border strips end to end on the diagonal to make a strip approximately 320" long. Trim the excess beyond the ¼" seam allowance and press the seams open.

Lay the quilt center on the floor, smoothing it gently. Do not tug or pull. Measure the quilt through the center from top to bottom. Cut the inner side borders this length. Sew the side borders to the quilt sides with right sides together, pinning to match centers and ends. Ease where necessary to fit. Press seams toward the borders.

Repeat for top and bottom borders, measuring across the quilt center, including the borders just added in the measurement. Cut the top and bottom borders this length. Stitch the top and bottom borders to the quilt center, pinning to match centers and ends, easing where necessary to fit. Press seams toward the borders.

Checkerboard Border

Side Borders

Join 37 four-patch units side by side into one long length for each side border. Press. Sew the checkerboard side borders to the quilt sides with right sides together, pinning to match centers and ends. Ease where necessary to fit. Press seams toward the inner borders.

Top and Bottom Borders

Join 33 four-patches side by side into one long length for each top and bottom border. Press. Add the top and bottom border in the same manner as the side borders.

Outer Border

Join the 8 blue border strips end to end on the straight of grain to make a strip approximately 320" long. Press the seams open. Add the outer borders in the same manner as the inner borders.

FINISHING

Winston Ways was machine quilted with antique gold thread and an edge-to-edge design called Deb's Swirls by Debra Geissler. Refer to the resources page for contact information.

Join the red scraps on the diagonal to make 360" of binding and bind.

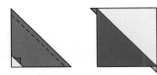

A Four-Patch Units

2 1/2" square unfinished

Make 620

B Half-Square Triangle Units

Blue/Neutral

2 1/2" square unfinished

Make 240

C Half-Square Triangle Units

Black/Gold

2 1/2" square unfinished

Make 360

D Winston Ways Block Construction

Winston Ways Block

12 1/2" square unfinished

Make 30

WINSTON WAYS

QUILT ASSEMBLY DIAGRAM

MIDNIGHT FLIGHT

QUILT STATISTICS
MADE BY BONNIE K. HUNTER
SIZE: 82" X 82"
BLOCK: 36 – 12" SQUARE FINISHED
INNER BORDER: 1" WIDE FINISHED
PIECED OUTER BORDER: 4" WIDE FINISHED

Challenges are good for helping us dig deeper and forcing us to try things a little bit outside of our usual "box of scrappy tricks." In the case of Midnight Flight, I was designing on my laptop during a red-eye flight home across the country after a teaching engagement. In the middle of the night my seat was lit by the glow from the laptop while everyone around me dozed.

As we neared our destination, dawn was breaking over the Eastern horizon and I had my block and quilt drawn and drafted and ready to begin - after I allowed myself to catch up on some much needed sleep! This block was designed for an issue of "100 blocks by 100 designers" by Quiltmaker Magazine, as was **Winston Ways** on page 68. The main "out of the box" part for me was the color scheme: Purple/Black/Cheddar and Red? Could I pull it off? I think I did!

FABRICS

Blocks and Pieced Outer Border
- 1 ½ yards of solid red
- 1 ⅝ yards of solid cheddar
- 4 yards of purple and blue scraps
- 1 ⅛ yards black scraps
- 5 ⅛ yards of neutral scraps for blocks

Inner Border
- ½ yard of black and white check

Binding
- ¾ yard of cheddar

CUTTING

Four-Patch Units
- From the red, cut 432 – 1 ½" squares
- From the cheddar, cut 432 – 1 ½" squares
- From the neutral scraps, cut 864 – 1 ½" squares

Half-Square Triangle Units
- From the black scraps, cut 144 – 2 ⅞" squares
- From the neutral scraps, cut 144 – 2 ⅞" squares

If using the Easy Angle ruler, cut black 2 ½" strips and neutral 2 ½" strips.

Star Blade Units
- From the purple and blue scraps, cut 288 – 2 ½" x 4 ½" rectangles
- From the neutral scraps, cut 576 – 2 ½" squares

Inner Border

- From the black and white check, cut 8 – 1 $\frac{1}{2}$" x the width of fabric strips
- From the red, cut 2 – 1 $\frac{1}{2}$" squares
- From the cheddar, cut 2 – 1 $\frac{1}{2}$" squares

Pieced Outer Border

- From purple and blue scraps, cut: 148 - 2 $\frac{1}{2}$" x 4 $\frac{1}{2}$" rectangles 4 – 2 $\frac{7}{8}$" squares for cornerstone half-square triangles
- From the red, cut: 148 – 2 $\frac{1}{2}$" squares 4 – 1 $\frac{1}{2}$" squares for the cornerstone four-patches
- From the cheddar, cut: 148 – 2 $\frac{1}{2}$" squares 4 – 1 $\frac{1}{2}$" squares for the cornerstones 4 – 2 $\frac{7}{8}$" squares for cornerstone half-square triangles 4 – 2 $\frac{1}{2}$" squares for cornerstone four-patches
- From the neutral, cut 8 – 1 $\frac{1}{2}$" squares for the cornerstone four-patches

Binding

From the cheddar, cut 10 – 2 $\frac{1}{2}$" x the width of fabric strips

Diagrams are on pages 78-79.

PIECING

Four-Patch Units

You can make your four-patches Leader and Ender style or use the strip piecing method found on page 13. When constructing the four-patches, make sure to spin the seams as shown on page 12. This ensures that no matter what direction you turn them, the seams will always nest together.

Four-patch construction

A Using 2 – 1 $\frac{1}{2}$" red squares and 2 – 1 $\frac{1}{2}$" neutral squares AND 2 – 1 $\frac{1}{2}$" cheddar squares and 2 – 1 $\frac{1}{2}$" neutral squares, make four-patch units as shown in the diagram. Repeat to make 218 red/neutral and 218 cheddar/neutral 2 $\frac{1}{2}$" units. Reserve 2 each for the border corner units.

Half-Square Triangle Units

Black /Neutral

B Layer the black squares and neutral squares with right sides together. Cut from corner to corner once on the diagonal to make 288 matched pairs. Stitch into 288

half-square triangle units, enough for 36 blocks. Press the seams toward the black fabric and trim the dog ears. Each block requires 8 black/neutral half-square triangle units.

If using the Easy Angle Ruler, place the black 2 $\frac{1}{2}$" strips and neutral 2 $\frac{1}{2}$" strips with right sides together. Using the 2" line on the ruler, cut the fabric into 288 matched pairs. Stitch the pairs together along the bias edge and press to the black. The units should measure 2 $\frac{1}{2}$" and finish at 2".

Star Blades

C-D Mark a diagonal line on the back side of each neutral square. Referring to the diagrams, place a square right-sides together, on one end of the rectangle, paying attention to which direction the lines go. Stitch on the drawn line and trim $\frac{1}{4}$" from the seam. Repeat with another square on the other end of the rectangle. Press. Make 144 Unit 1 and 144 Unit 2.

Block Quarter Assembly

E Lay out 3 cheddar four-patch units, 2 half-square triangle units and 1 Unit 1 and 1 Unit 2 rectangle. Sew 2 cheddar four-patches and 2 half-square triangle units into a four-patch. Sew the remaining four-patch to the Unit 1 rectangle and sew the Unit 2 rectangle to the side of the large unit. Sew the units together to complete the block quarter. Press. Repeat to make 72 yellow quarter blocks and 72 red quarter blocks. Block quarters will measure 6 $\frac{1}{2}$" square and finish at 6".

F Arrange 4 block quarters as shown. Join together to complete one block. Press. Make 36 blocks.

Quilt Top Center Assembly

Referring to the quilt assembly diagram, lay out the blocks in 6 rows of 6 blocks each. Stitch the quilt center into rows. Join the rows to complete the quilt top center. Press.

Borders

Inner Border

Join the 8 border strips end to end with diagonal seams to make a strip approximately 320" long. Trim the excess beyond the $\frac{1}{4}$" seam allowance and press the seams open.

Lay the quilt center out on the floor, smoothing it gently. Do not tug or pull. Measure the quilt through the center from top to bottom. Cut 4 inner borders this length.

Sew the inner side borders to the quilt sides with right sides together, pinning to match centers and ends. Ease where necessary to fit. Press seams toward the borders.

Add a red cornerstone and a cheddar cornerstone to each end of the top and bottom inner borders. Press seams toward the border. Sew top and bottom borders to the quilt, placing one red corner stone at the upper left of the quilt top and the lower right of the quilt bottom. The opposite corners, upper right and lower left will have cheddar cornerstones. Press.

Pieced Outer Border

G As with the star blade units, mark a diagonal line on the back side of each cheddar and red square. Referring to the diagrams on page 79, place 2 squares right-sides together, on a rectangle, paying attention to which direction the lines go. Stitch on the drawn line and trim the excess beyond the 1/4" seam allowance. Press the seams open. Make 74 Border Unit 1 and 74 Border Unit 2.

H-I These borders may look the same, but there is a slight difference – the units are placed to turn the corners correctly. The side borders make a zigzag at the right end; the top and bottom borders do the zigzag at the left. Make sure you label them correctly so they turn the corners correctly.

Sew the units together as shown and press. Sew the side borders to the quilt sides with right sides together, pinning to match centers and ends. Ease where necessary to fit. Press seams toward the inner border.

Border Corners

J Make 8 half-square triangles as shown. Layer the cheddar squares and purple/blue squares with right sides together. Cut from corner to corner once on the diagonal to yield 8 matched pairs. Stitch into 8 half-square triangle units. Press the seams toward the purple/blue fabric and trim the dog ears. Make 8. Units are 2 1/2" unfinished and finish at 2".

Lay out 2 half-square triangles, 1 reserved four-patch unit and 1 plain cheddar square. Sew into pairs and join the pairs. Press. Make 2 in each colorway. Units will measure 4 1/2" square unfinished and finish at 4".

K Sew a border corner to each end of the pieced top and bottom borders, paying attention to which cornerstone in the inner border these pieced units are going to chain into. The corner with the cheddar four-patch should chain to the cheddar cornerstone in the inner border and the red to the red. Press.

Join top and bottom borders to the quilt, pinning to match centers and ends, easing where necessary to fit. Press toward the inner border.

FINISHING

Midnight Flight was quilted with lavender thread in an edge-to-edge design called Deb's Feathers by Deb Geissler. Refer to the resources page for contact information.

A cheddar binding finishes the quilt.

A Four-Patch Units
2 1/2" square unfinished
Make 218 red/neutral
Make 218 cheddar/neutral

B Half-Square Triangle Units
Black/Neutral
2 1/2" square unfinished
Make 288

Unit 1   Unit 2

C Star Blade Construction

  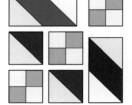  

Unit 1   Unit 2

D Star Blades
2 1/2" x 4 1/2" unfinished
Make 144 Star
Blade Unit 1
Make 144 Star
Blade Unit 2

E Quarter Block Assembly
Make 72 block quarters
with cheddar chains and
72 with red chains.

F Midnight Flight Block
12" square unfinished
Make 36

G Border Units
2 1/2" x 4 1/2"
Make 74 Border
Unit 1
and 74 Border
Unit 2

Zig-zag

▲ **H Side Borders**
Note that the side borders are different
from the top and bottom borders.
Make 2

▼ **I Top and Bottom Borders**
Note that the left end is different from the
side borders.
Make 2

Zig-zag

J Border Corner Half-Square Triangles
2 1/2" square unfinished
Make 8

K Border Corner Units
4 1/2" square unfinished
Make 2 in each colorway

MIDNIGHT FLIGHT

EASY STREET

QUILT STATISTICS
MADE BY BONNIE K.HUNTER
SIZE: 96" X 96"
16 BLOCK A – 15" SQUARE FINISHED
9 BLOCK B – 15" SQUARE FINISHED
INNER BORDER: 1" WIDE FINISHED
OUTER BORDER: 4 ¹/₂" WIDE FINISHED

If you ever dreamed you'd find yourself on Easy Street, this just might be the quilt for you! The blocks are large at 15" square, and the units all finish at 3" each, so it is easy to construct – well worth the time it takes to do so.

Easy Street is an "on-point" setting with pieced setting triangles that fool the eye a little bit, making it a fun one to put together from cool tropical colored scraps.

FABRICS

Blocks

- 2 ¹/₄ yards total of bright lime/ apple green scraps
- 1 ¹/₂ yards total of cool aqua and turquoise scraps
- 1 ³/₄ yards total of assorted purple scraps
- 1 ¹/₂ yards of gray
- 4 yards of black-on-white prints

Borders

- ¹/₂ yard of fuchsia
- 1 ¹/₂ yards of turquoise print

Binding

- ⁷/₈ yard of dark purple print

CUTTING

Four Patch Units

- From the gray, cut 384 – 2" squares.
- From the black-on-white prints, cut 384 – 2" squares.

Flying Geese Units

- From the purple, cut 48 – 4 ¹/₄" squares.
- From the black-on-white prints, cut 128 – 2 ³/₈" squares.
- From turquoise, cut 64 – 2 ³/₈" squares.

Split Triangle Units

- From the turquoise, cut 32 – 3 ⁷/₈" squares. Cut each in half on the diagonal to make 64 triangles.
- From the black on white prints, cut 64 – 2 ³/₈" squares. Cut each in half on the diagonal to make 128 wing triangles.
- From the purple, cut 64 – 2" squares.

Double Brick Units

From the black-on-white prints, cut 2" strips. Subcut the strips into 3 ¹/₂" rectangles to make 320— 2" x 3 ¹/₂" rectangles.

Square Units

- From the green prints, cut 169 – 3 1/2" squares.
- From the purple, cut 16 – 3 1/2" squares.

Star Point Units

- From the turquoise, cut 64 – 3 1/2" squares.
- From the purple, cut 128 – 2" squares.

Setting Triangles

- From the green, cut:
  19 – 5 1/2" squares. Cut each in half on the diagonal twice with an X to make 76 quarter square triangles.
- 2 – 3" squares. Cut each in half on the diagonal to make 4 corner triangles.

Borders

- From the fuschia, cut 9 – 1 1/2" x the width of fabric strips.
- From the turquoise print, cut 10 – 5" x the width of fabric strips.

Binding

- From the purple, cut 11 – 2 1/2" x the width of fabric strips.

Diagrams are on page 86-87.

PIECING

Four-Patch Units

All of the 192 four-patches for this quilt were made as Leaders and Enders while I was assembling the other block parts. While the black-on-white prints are a newer acquisition, the gray fabric had been sitting in the stash since 1992!

You can make the four patches Leader and Ender style or use the strip piecing method found on page 13. When constructing the four patches, make sure to spin the seams as shown on page 12. This ensures that no matter what direction you turn them, the seams will always nest together.

Four patch construction

A Using 2 – 2" black-on-white print squares and 2 – 2" gray squares, make a four-patch unit as shown in the diagram. Repeat to make 192 – 3 1/2" units.

Flying Geese Units

B-C There is a whole flock of geese in this quilt! Each Block A has 4 purple/white and 4 purple/turquoise geese units. Each Block B has 4 purple/white geese units. You can use any method that gives you a flying geese unit that finishes at 1 1/2" x 3". The method shown here will give you 4 matching geese from each set of squares.

I used the Easy Angle Ruler and 2" strips for the half-square "wing" triangles for the flying geese units, and more 2" strips and the Companion Angle Ruler for the larger quarter-square triangle "goose" part of the flying geese units in this quilt.

The method shown using 4 1/4" and 2 3/8" squares is given as an option for those who don't have access to these rulers.

Flying Geese Construction

D To make 4 identical flying geese units, you'll need 1 large 4 1/4" square and 4 small 2 3/8" squares.

E With right sides together, lay 2 black-on-white 2 3/8" squares on top of 1 purple 4 1/4" square so the small squares line up with the top left and lower right corners and overlap in the center. Draw a diagonal line through the small squares as shown. Sew a scant 1/4" on each side of the drawn line and cut apart on the line.

F Press the unit open with the seams away from the small triangles.

G Place another small square in the corner of the geese triangle, with right sides together. Draw a diagonal line on the back of the small square. Sew a scant 1/4" on each side of the marked line and cut apart on the line. Press seams to the triangle to make 4 flying geese units. Repeat, using 32 total 4 1/4" purple squares and 128 total 2 3/8" black-on-white squares to make 128 purple/black-on-white flying geese units.

Using remaining 16 large purple squares and the 64 small turquoise squares, make 64 purple/turquoise flying geese units.

Flying Geese Pairs

H Stitch a purple/black-on-white flying geese unit on top of a purple/turquoise unit. Press. Make 64 units. Set remaining 64 purple/black-on-white geese aside.

Split Triangle Units

I With right sides together stitch a wing triangle to 2 adjacent sides of a purple square as shown. Press seams away from the square.

Match a pieced triangle unit with a turquoise triangle to make 1 split triangle unit. Press toward the turquoise triangle. Make 64.

Double Brick Units

You can make the double brick units Leader and Ender style or use the strip piecing method found on page 13 to make the double units.

Double Brick Construction

J Stitch pairs of 2" x 3 1/2" black-on-white rectangles with right sides together. Press seams to one side. Make 128 units. Set remaining 64 bricks aside.

Geese and Brick Unit

K Gather the remaining purple/black-on-white geese and black-on-white bricks. Stitch a 2" x 3 1/2" black-on-white brick to the top of a purple/black-on-white flying geese unit. Press seams to the brick. Make 64 – 36 for Block B and 28 for the setting triangles.

Star Point Units

L-M Draw a diagonal line on the back of each purple square from corner to corner. Place a square in the corner or each base block with right sides together as shown. Stitch from corner to corner across the green square following the line. Fold the triangle back to be sure it meets the edge of the base square. Press and trim excess. Repeat for the second star point. Make 64 – 36 for Block B and 28 for the setting triangles.

Block Construction

Block A

Each Block A block consists of 4 four patch units, 8 double brick units, 4 double flying geese units, 4 split triangle units, 4 plain green squares and 1 plain purple square.

N Lay out the units as shown in the diagram. Pay close attention to which direction the four patches and the seams on the double brick units are facing. Stitch the block units into rows and join rows to complete the block. Press. Make 16.

Block B

Each Block B block consists of 8 four patch units, 4 geese and brick units, 9 plain green squares and 4 star point units.

O Lay out the units as shown. Pay close attention to which direction the four patches and the seams on the double brick units are facing. Stitch the block units into rows and join rows to complete the block. Press. Make 9.

Setting Triangles

Each setting triangle is made of 4 four patch units, 2 geese and brick units, 2 star point units, 2 green plain squares and 5 green quarter square triangles.

P Join units into rows and join rows to complete triangle. Press. Make 12.

Corner Triangles

The corner triangles consist of 2 four patch units, 1 geese and brick unit, 1 star point unit, 4 quarter square triangles and 1 corner triangle.

Q Join the units into rows and join rows to complete triangle. Press. Make 4.

Quilt Top Assembly

Easy Street is an on-point setting, and assembled in diagonal rows. Referring to the quilt assembly diagram lay out the blocks filling in the sides with the setting triangles and corners. I like to piece diagonally set quilts into two halves. With this quilt, one half will be larger than the other because it is a square quilt. This keeps things from being too unwieldy, especially when sewing a large quilt top. Join quilt top halves to complete quilt center. Press.

Borders

Inner Border

Join the 9 fuchsia border strips end to end on the diagonal to make a strip approximately 360" long. Trim the excess beyond the 1/4" seam allowance and press the seams open.

Lay the quilt center on the floor, smoothing it gently. Do not tug or pull. Measure the quilt through the center from top to bottom. Cut the inner side borders this length. Sew the side borders to the quilt sides with right sides

together, pinning to match centers and ends. Ease where necessary to fit. Press seams toward the borders. Repeat for top and bottom borders, measuring across the quilt center, including the borders just added in the measurement. Cut the top and bottom borders this length. Stitch the top and bottom borders to the quilt center, pinning to match centers and ends, easing where necessary to fit. Press seams toward borders.

Outer Border

Join the 10 outer border strips end to end on the straight of grain to make a strip approximately 360" long. Press seams open. Add the outer borders in the same manner as the inner borders.

FINISHING

Easy Street was machine quilted with a pastel variegated thread in an edge-to-edge design called Two-Fold Feathers by Hermione Agee of Lorien Quilting. Refer to the resources page for contact information.

Make 440" of binding with the dark purple fabric and bind.

B Flying Geese Units
Purple/Black-on
White Print
2" x 3 1/2" unfinished
Make 128

C Flying Geese Units
Purple/Turquoise
2" x 3 1/2" unfinished
Make 64

A Four Patch Units
3 1/2" square
unfinished
Make 192

D-G FlyingGeese Construction

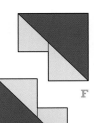

**H Flying
Geese Pairs**
3 1/2" square
unfinished
Make 64

E   F   G

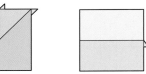

**◄ L Star Point Unit
Construction**

I Split Triangle Units
3 1/2" square unfinished
Make 64

**J Double
Brick Units**
3 1/2" square
unfinished
Make 128

**K Geese and
Brick Unit**
3 1/2" square
unfinished
Make 64

M Star Point Units
3 1/2" square unfinished
Make 64

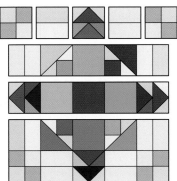

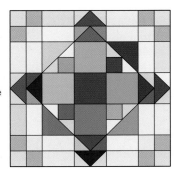

N Block A
15 1/2" square
unfinished
Make 16

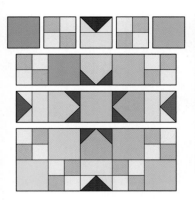

O Block B

15 ½" square unfinished

Make 9

P Side Setting Triangle

Make 12

**Q Corner
Setting Triangle**

Make 4

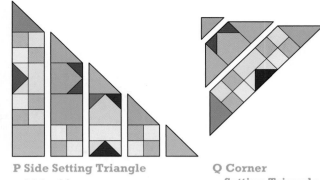

QUILT ASSEMBLY DIAGRAM

LAZY SUNDAY

QUILT STATISTICS
MADE BY BONNIE K. HUNTER
SIZE: 76" X 96"
LAZY LADDER BLOCK: 24 – 9" SQUARE FINISHED
SUNDAY STAR BLOCK: 24 – 9" SQUARE FINISHED
INNER BORDER: 1 ¹/₂" WIDE FINISHED
PIECED OUTER BORDER: 6" WIDE FINISHED

I love playing with bright colors. Hot pink, orange, green, purple and turquoise – they are such happy colors. And as always, I use lots of different background neutrals for variety. There are many pieces in this quilt, but it is so worth it to take the time and put it all in, even the border. The sewing is easy – just take it one step at a time.

FABRICS

- 1 ¹/₄ yards total of turquoise scraps for the blocks, cornerstones and binding
- 1 ³/₈ yards total of green scraps for the blocks and border
- 1 ³/₈ yards total of orange scraps for the blocks and border
- 1 ¹/₄ yards total of pink scraps for the blocks and border
- 2 ³/₈ yards total of purple scraps for the blocks and border
- 5 yards of neutral scraps for the blocks, sashing and borders

CUTTING

Lazy Ladder Blocks

Half-Square Triangle Units
- From the green scraps, cut 48 – 3 ⁷/₈" squares
- From the neutral scraps, cut 48 – 3 ⁷/₈" squares

If using the Easy Angle Ruler, cut green 3 ¹/₂" strips and neutral 3 ¹/₂" strips.

Four-Patch Units
- From the purple scraps, cut 48 – 2" squares
- From the neutral scraps, cut 96 – 2" squares
- From the pink scraps, cut 144 – 2" squares
- From purple scraps, cut 48 – 3 ¹/₂" squares

Sunday Star Blocks

Pieced Square Units
- From the pink scraps, cut 96 – 2" squares
- From the green scraps, cut 4 – 2 ³/₈" squares. Slice each square once from corner to corner on the diagonal to yield 8 wing triangles.
- From the neutral scraps, cut 46 – 2 ³/₈" squares. Slice each square once from corner to corner on the diagonal to yield 92 wing triangles.

Quarter-Square Star Points

- From the orange scraps, cut 48 – 4 $1/4$" squares
- From the pink scraps, cut 24 – 4 $1/4$" squares
- From the neutral scraps, cut 24 – 4 $1/4$" squares

Center Squares

- From From the turquoise scraps, cut 24 – 3 $1/2$" center squares

> If using the Companion Angle Ruler, cut quarter-square triangles from 2" strips

Sashing

- From the neutral scraps, cut 110 – 1 $1/2$" x 9 $1/2$" rectangles
- From the turquoise scraps, cut 63 – 1 $1/2$" squares for cornerstones

Inner Border

- From the orange scraps, cut 2" wide strips in various lengths.

Outer Border

Diamond in a Rectangle Unit
- From the purple scraps, cut 156 – 2 $1/2$" x 4 $1/2$" rectangles
- From the neutral scraps, cut 312 – 2 $1/2$" squares

Half-Square Triangle Units
- From the green scraps, cut 74 – 2 $7/8$" squares
- From the neutral scraps, cut 74 – 2 $7/8$" squares

Border Corner Blocks
From the neutral scraps, cut:
- 4 – 2 $1/2$" squares. Draw a diagonal line from corner to corner on the back side of each square.
- 4 – 2 $7/8$" squares

From the purple scraps, cut:
- 4 – 2 $1/2$" squares
- 4 – 2 $7/8$" squares
- From the green scraps, cut 4 – 2 $1/2$" squares

Binding

- From the turquoise, cut 10 – 2 $1/2$" x the width of fabric strips

Diagrams are on pages 93-94.

PIECING

Lazy Ladder Block

Half-Square Triangles Units

A Layer the green squares and neutral squares with right sides together. Cut from corner to corner once on the diagonal to yield 96 matched pairs. Stitch into 96 half-square triangle units. Press the seams toward the green fabric and trim the dog ears.

> If using the Easy Angle Ruler, place the green strips and neutral strips with right sides together. Using the 3" line on the ruler, cut the strips into 96 matched pairs. Stitch the pairs together along the bias edge and press to the green. The units should measure 3 $1/2$" and finish at 3".

Four-Patch Units
All of the four-patches for this quilt were made as Leaders and Enders while I was assembling the other block parts. You can make your four-patches Leader and Ender style or use the strip piecing method found on page 13. When constructing the four-patches, make sure to spin the seams as shown on page 12. This ensures that no matter what direction you turn them, the seams will always nest together.

Four-patch construction
B Using 2 – 2" pink squares and 2 –2" neutral squares, make a four-patch unit as shown in the diagram. Repeat to make 48 – 3 $1/2$" units. Using the remaining pink and purple squares, make 24 four-patch units.

Lazy Ladder Block Assembly
C Sew the units into 3 rows of 3 units, making sure the chains are going in the right direction. Join the rows to complete the block. Press. Make 24 Lazy Ladder Blocks that are 9 $1/2$" square unfinished.

Sunday Star Block

Pieced Square Units

D Stitch a green wing triangle to both sides of a pink corner square. Press the seams toward the triangles. Repeat to make 4 pieced triangle units.

Stitch a neutral wing triangle to 2 adjacent sides of a pink corner square. Press the seams toward the triangles. Repeat to make 92 pieced triangle units.

Remove the dog ears at the center of the unit.

E Match a pieced triangle unit with a large pink triangle and stitch. Press to the large triangle. Make 4 units with green wings and 92 with neutral wings. Remove the dog ears. Units will measure 3 $^1/_2$" square unfinished and will finish at 3".

Quarter-Square Star Point Units

F-G Layer the 24 pink and 24 of the orange squares with right sides together in pairs. Slice the pairs of squares from corner to corner twice with an X to yield 96 quarter square triangle pairs.

Layer the 24 neutral and the remaining 24 orange squares with right sides together in pairs. Slice pairs of squares from corner to corner twice with an X to yield 96 quarter-square triangle pairs.

Stitch the quarter-square triangles into half units as shown. Press the seams toward the orange triangles. Join the half units together to make 96 star point units.

For the quarter-square units in this block, I placed 2" orange and pink strips right sides together, and 2" orange and neutral strips right sides together, using the companion angle ruler to cut them into already-matched pairs, ready to feed through the machine. Join an orange/pink half-hourglass to a neutral/orange half-hourglass to complete the unit. See diagram F. The units will measure 3 $^1/_2$" square and finish at 3" in the block.

Sunday Star Block Assembly

H Referring to the diagram, arrange the units as shown, making sure the chains are going in the right direction. Sew the units into rows. Join the rows to complete the block. Press. Make 24 Sunday Star Blocks. Blocks will measure 9 $^1/_2$" unfinished and finish at 9".

Quilt Top Center Assembly

Referring to the quilt assembly diagram on page 94, lay out the blocks in rows along with the sashing pieces and the turquoise cornerstones making sure the chains in the secondary pattern are going in the right directions. Stitch the quilt center into rows, pressing the seams toward the sashing, away from the cornerstones. Join the rows to complete the quilt top center. Press.

BORDERS

Inner border

Join the strips end to end into a strip approximately 306" long. Press seams open. Lay the quilt center out on the floor, smoothing it gently. Do not tug or pull. Measure the quilt through the center from top to bottom. Cut the inner borders to this length. Sew the side borders to the quilt sides with right sides together, pinning to match centers and ends. Ease where necessary to fit. Press the seams toward the borders.

Repeat for the top and bottom borders, measuring across the quilt center from side to side, including the borders just added in the measurement. Cut the top and bottom borders this length. Stitch the top and bottom borders to the quilt center, pinning to match centers and ends, easing where necessary to fit. Press seams toward the borders.

Pieced Outer Border

Diamond in a Rectangle Unit
I-J Referring to the diagrams on page 93, place 2 squares right-sides together, on a rectangle, paying attention to which direction the lines go. Stitch on the drawn line and trim $1/4$" from the seam. Press. Make 78 Unit 1 and 78 Unit 2. The units will measure $2 1/2$" x $4 1/2$" and finish at 2" x 4" in the quilt.

K Layer the green squares and neutral squares with right sides together. Cut from corner to corner once on the diagonal to yield 148 matched pairs. Stitch into 148 half-square triangle units. Press the seams toward the green fabric and trim dog ears.

Left Side Border

I found it easiest to build each border length in halves, one using Unit 1 diamonds and one using Unit 2 diamonds. Then join the halves to complete each border length.

L Join 21 Unit 2 diamonds side by side. Press the seams toward the left. Join 21 half-square triangles side by side as shown. Press the seams toward the right. Join the diamond and half-square triangle border lengths together into one outer side border half.

Right Side Border

M Repeat using 21 Unit 1 diamonds and 21 half-square triangles. Join the two outer side border halves together as shown. Make 2 outer side borders.

Top and Bottom Borders

The top and bottom borders are made the same way as the side borders, with each having 16 Unit 1 rectangles and 16 Unit 2 rectangles. Make 2.

You will have 8 leftover diamond in a rectangle units that will be used in making the border corner blocks below.

Border Corner Blocks

Half-Square Triangle Units
From the neutral and purple squares, make 8 half-square triangle units as shown in Diagram A on the next page.

N Lay out 2 half-square triangle units, 1 neutral square and 1 purple square and sew together as shown in the diagram on page 93. Press to the plain squares.

O Lay out 2 reserved diamond in a rectangle units (a Unit 1 and a Unit 2), 1 border corner unit and 1 green square as shown in the diagram on page 93. Sew together. Press. Make 4.

Referring to the quilt assembly diagram on page 94, join the corner blocks to each end of the top and bottom borders, making sure they are going in the correct direction. Add the top and bottom borders to quilt, pinning to match centers and ends and easing where necessary to fit.

FINISHING

Lazy Sunday is machine quilted with Signature "Pastels" thread in an edge-to-edge design called Twofold Feathers by Hermione Agee of Lorien Quilting. Refer to the resources page for contact information.

The quilt is bound in turquoise to bring the coolness of the star block centers and the cornerstones to the outside edge of the quilt.

A Half-Square Triangle Units
3 $1/2$" square unfinished
Make 96

B Four-Patch Units
3 $1/2$" square unfinished
Make 48 pink/neutral
Make 24 pink/purple

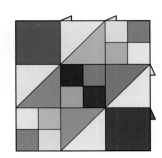

C Lazy Ladder Block
9 $1/2$" square unfinished
Make 24

D Pieced Triangle Units
Make 4 with green wing triangles
Make 92 with neutral wing triangles

E Pieced Square Units
3 $1/2$" square unfinished
Make 4 with green wings
Make 92 with neutral wings

F Quarter-Square Star Point Construction
Make 96 pink/orange
Make 96 pink/neutral

G Quarter-Square Star Points
3 $1/2$" unfinished
Make 96

 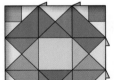

H Sunday Star Block
9 $1/2$" square unfinished
Make 4 with green corner unit
Make 20 with neutral corner units

Unit 1   Unit 2

I Diamond in a Rectangle Construction

Unit 1   Unit 2

J Diamond in a Rectangle Units
2 $1/2$" x 4 $1/2$" rectangles unfinished
Make 78 Unit 1
Make 78 Unit 2

K Half-Square Triangle Units
2 $1/2$" square unfinished
Make 148

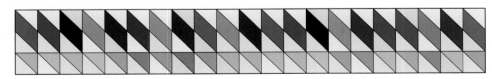

L Left Side Border
Make 2

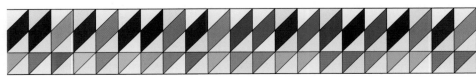

M Right Side Border
Make 2

N Border Corner Unit
4 ¹/₂" unfinished
Make 4

O Border Corner
6 ¹/₂" square unfinished
Make 4

QUILT ASSEMBLY DIAGRAM

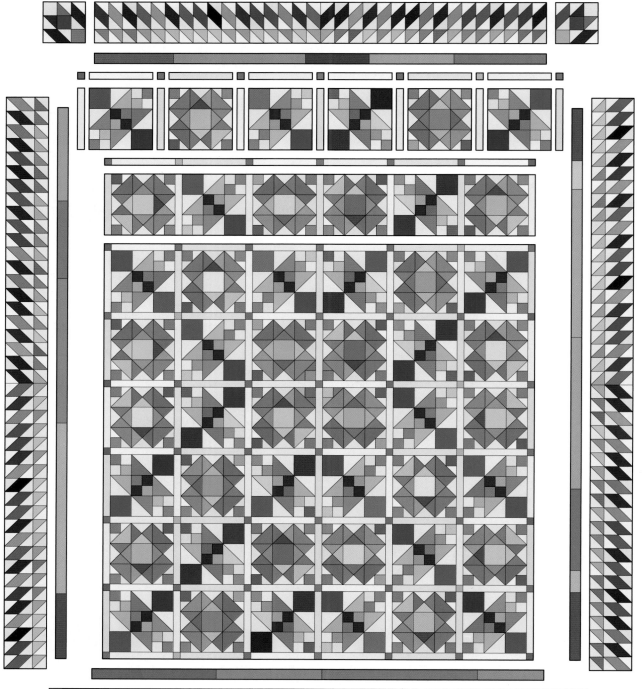

ABOUT THE AUTHOR

Bonnie K. Hunter is passionate about quilting, focusing mainly on scrap quilts with the simple feeling of "making do." She started her love affair with quilting in a home economics class her senior year of high school in 1980 and has never looked back. Before quilting became her full time career, Bonnie was the owner and designer of Needle in a Haystack!! creating more than 70 patterns for dolls and stuffed animals with a country primitive feel.

Many of her designs were licensed through the Butterick Pattern Company, translated into seven languages and sold around the globe through fabric stores. But quilting has always been Bonnie's first love. She has been machine quilting since 1989 and professionally long arm quilting for the public since 1995, retiring in 2009 when she no longer had the time due to her teaching, traveling and writing schedule. She has been featured in magazines both for her quilt patterns and articles she has written on scrap management and using that stash to its full potential.

Dedicated to continuing the traditions of quilting, Bonnie enjoys meeting with quilters, teaching workshops and lecturing to quilt guilds all over the world, challenging quilters to break the rules, think outside the box, and find what brings them joy. Bonnie received Best Teacher, Author, Designer, Best New Book Release and Lifetime Achievement awards in 2013 through a global Internet poll hosted via Sew Cal Gal, and was completely flabbergasted, not to mention honored and humbled at the same time.

When not traveling and teaching, she spends her time piecing scrap quilts, enjoying the peaceful reward of English paper piecing and hand quilting as much as machine work, and loving life in her wooded surroundings in beautiful rural Wallburg, N.C., a suburb of Winston-Salem. She and her husband, Dave are the proud parents of two grown sons, Jason and Jeffrey. They round out their household with Sadie the dog and two cats – Emmy Lou, who loves life inside only, and Chloe who only loves life on the outside. Both keep Bonnie company while she designs, quilts and plays happily with her fabric. She spends time with her vintage sewing machine collection and considers piecing on an antique treadle machine as workout time well spent!

When she has a chance, she escapes to the beautiful Blue Ridge Mountains to spend quilting get-away time in her mountain cabin affectionately and half-jokingly named Quilt Villa. Bonnie also writes a regular column for **Quiltmaker** magazine entitled "Addicted to Scraps" with the main intention to help you to put various aspects of your own Scrap Users System to good use! Catch up with Bonnie's doings through her extensive website at www.Quiltville.com. There you will find Quiltville's calendar for lectures and workshops, tips and tricks, techniques, tutorials and a long list of free quilt patterns to help you dig into your scraps.

From there, head over to www.Quiltville.blogspot.com for Bonnie's (almost) daily blog, Quiltville's Quips & Snips. Her global email list, Quiltvillechat, found at groups.yahoo.com/group/quiltvillechat has become a hot spot for mystery quilters from all over the world with a focus on using scraps and stash.

And keep in real-time touch with Bonnie and her community of "Quiltvillians" on the Quiltville Friends Page. www.Facebook.com/QuiltvilleFriends

Bonnie's favorite motto? "The Best Things in Life are Quilted!" of course!

Specialty Rulers:
EZ Quilting by Wrights
Phone: (800) 660-0415
Email: help@wrights.com
Website: www.ezquilt.com

Quilting Designs:
Patricia E Ritter, Urban Elementz
125 Sunny Creek
New Braunfels, TX 78132
Phone (830) 964-6133
Email: patricia@urbanelementz.com
Website: www.urbanelementz.com

Hermoine Agee, Lorien Quilting
30 Lockwood Rd.
Belgrave Heights 3160 VIC Australia
Phone: (03) 9754 4916
Email hermione@lorienquilting.com
Website: www.lorienquilting.com

Gali Design:
Jodi Beamish of Gali Design at
Willow Leaf Studio
Phone: (888) 945-5695
Email: wlscontact@gmail.com
Website: www.willowleafstudio.com

Debra Giessler, Designs By Deb
Email: dgeissler@comcast.net
Website: www.debrageissler.com

TRY THESE

Look for Bonnie's other books for more scrap quilt inspiration!